CW00500570

THE SOUL

Piers Morris

Grosvenor House
Publishing Limited

All rights reserved
Copyright © Piers Morris, 2020

The right of Piers Morris to be identified as the author of this work has been asserted in accordance with Section 78 of the Copyright, Designs and Patents Act 1988

The book cover is copyright to Piers Morris

This book is published by
Grosvenor House Publishing Ltd
Link House
140 The Broadway, Tolworth, Surrey, KT6 7HT.
www.grosvenorhousepublishing.co.uk

A CIP record for this book
is available from the British Library

ISBN 978-1-83975-306-0

We read to know we are not alone
C. S. Lewis

AUTHOR NOTE

Piers Morris is a British solicitor who worked as an international project lawyer for more than three decades across over 100 countries around the world.

In 2015 he published a summary of the key literature on extraterrestrial existence, alien life and UFOs, entitled *They Exist.*

His first book, in 2010, was a project risk manual, *Risk in Business*, based on the successful business formula used in developing projects internationally.

Contents

PART 1:

THE DEVELOPMENT OF THE SOUL

Soul

What is a soul? In this book, a 'soul' is a spiritual entity which is temporarily housed within a human body and which survives the death of that body. It is not, however, composed of matter or of any other component of the physical world. It is an immortal unit of energy and awareness that cannot perish but can, and does, download itself into physical matter for periods of time.

The soul's creation from Source, its development, the journeys to and from the non-physical realm, and its merger back with Source, is explained in the pages that follow. The downloading into physicality requires the lowering of the soul's vibration as it moves out of the non-physical dimension and into the physical dimension. The return journey back into the non-physical realm is easier as the human body and all attachments are shed and the soul enters a lighter dimension where its vibration rises again.

This unit of energy, which can be perceived in a range of different colours in the non-physical realm, contains the essential ingredient of awareness, consciousness or 'spirit', which is often referred to as 'mind'. The mind will guide us both in life and on death.

This has nothing to do with the human brain, or the human body. The physical human body has a limited life span, but the soul and mind always survives the death of the human body that hosts it for a lifetime.

Purpose

Most of us are searching for a meaning and purpose in life that goes beyond physical maintenance and personal gratification. Much of the search for meaning and purpose in life has been focused on the idea that life in some form continues after physical death, and that unseen forces shape worlds and beings.

The sources referenced throughout this book reveal that the meaning and purpose of life is to develop our soul. We need to know that there is a reason, a purpose as to why we are here. The greatest philosophers have puzzled over the meaning and purpose of life, including Søren Kierkegaard, the 19th century Danish philosopher, who wrote:

Where am I? Who am I? How did I come here? What is this thing called the world? How did I come into the world? Why was I not consulted? And if I am compelled to take part in it, where is the manager? I would like to see him.

The soul starts its existence without a 'physical body' and, for this reason, we must understand the importance of the mind, as it is the part of 'us' that survives after the body dies. The sages, adepts and masters tell us that the tools we need for development are, in fact, *all contained within our mind.* Consequently, the mind is the key to understanding existence in physical and non-physical form.

In David Wilcock's *The Synchronicity Key* (2013), he references a sequence from the film *The Matrix* (1999) which reveals that the mind is the key, not material objects. In a sequence from the film, a young student of the Oracle says to Neo:

ORACLE STUDENT: Do not try and bend the spoon. That's impossible. Instead....only try to realise the truth.

NEO: What truth?

STUDENT: There is no spoon.

NEO: There is no spoon?

STUDENT: Then you'll see that it is not the spoon that bends – it is only yourself.

In Richard Matheson's 1978 novel *What Dreams May Come*, about survival after death, the newly-deceased subject arrives in 'heaven' and asks his guide where he is, wanting to know what country and state it was, as it was so beautiful. The guide smiles and said the place he was in was "a state of mind". Where we go after death is simply a state of mind - or rather, the state of mind we are in at that time.

The mind is the key

This is repeated time and time again in Matheson's novel. The mind is the key. In his introduction, Matheson says only one aspect of his classic story is fictional: the characters and relationships. The main detail of the book, however, was derived exclusively from research into the afterlife. The afterlife is "a world of existence where thought is king". This was the conclusion of the well-known physician Dr Kenneth Ring in his book *Life at Death*, as a result of his work with near-death patients.

Even the Bible is clear that everything started from the mind. Mind-before-matter, not, as scientists tell us, matter-before-mind. The Bible states, on the first page, that nothing existed in the beginning, no earth, no sun. In the absence of matter, space and time, what caused the creation of matter to occur? Something must have happened before there was anything. Since there was no *thing* (nothing) when something first happened, what could that event have been? It must have been a *mental* event. This is the basis of life and death. The key to both life and death is *in the mind*.

Regressive Life-between-Life hypnotherapy practitioners understand that the mind is the key when taking a client through the stage between life and death. Where the client (under hypnosis) is struggling to move into the spirit realm, the afterlife, or move around after leaving the body, they ask the client to talk to their personal guide, who is always nearby, and that guide will calm their mind, turn up 'the light in their mind' so they can 'see', and take them to their destination. This is how it is when we actually die.

Scientists naturally would not agree with the view that we have souls that survive death (or that there is an afterlife) as they cannot put a spirit or soul under a microscope and examine it, prod it, or jolt it with electric cables, so in their view it cannot be "real".

However, we have learnt breakthrough information from other sources in recent years which shows that the soul (and the afterlife) is in fact very real. The survival of the soul after bodily death has been shown through vast amounts of testimony which has been gathered from people who have undergone "near-death" experiences, pre-death experiences, experienced irrefutable communications with the dead, and through hypnosis, which recorded past life and inter-life experiences carried out under clinical conditions with experienced professionals.

Additionally, of course, we have the recollections of dimensional travelling by sages and masters and the rebirth memories of those masters and adepts who "lucidly died". These are all referenced in the pages that follow, including a remarkable source (Barham & Greene's *The Silver Cord)* where entities from the spirit realm *actually materialised* to provide information about the afterlife and the way in which the soul develops.

Numerous sources referenced in this book state that souls must complete a process of learning in a physical body before the need to physically incarnate ceases. The sooner we can complete that process and circumvent the need for 're-embodiment', the better. However, the learning curve is steep and the process fraught with dangers, temptations, cul-de-sacs and inappropriate choices due to the fact that humans have the right to exercise 'free will'.

The physical 'road test'

Our soul development or advancement, in other words, our level of consciousness, is a culmination of all our previous experience. We need the experience of life on Earth to test our progress. We might be able to work on spiritual advancement while in the non-physical spirit realm, but we need to 'road test' our advancement. One 'tour' of Earth is unlikely to be adequate to obtain all the range of experiences and learning necessary for spiritual advancement, which is why the design of reincarnation exists.

The need to return for further 'tours' is made more likely by the fact that life for the current version of the human on Earth has been compromised. Control of humans is now almost complete, and spirituality has largely been lost. To advance, we need to rediscover spirituality, and in this respect we will be assisted by the coming spiritual changes. Details of the spiritual war being fought at this time are referenced in Appendices 3 and 4.

It is often difficult for a soul to keep returning to Earth. Our life as a soul in the spirit realm is so beautiful that some souls simply don't want to be required to advance their learning in the physical Earth environment. The accomplished regression hypnotherapist, Susan Wisehart, in her book *Soul Visioning*, which is further referenced later, discusses the case of one client who she regressed back into the life-between-life state. This client was resisting the need to return to Earth for further learning, and needed significant persuasion from her spiritual counsellors. The counsellors stated:

"*You need to go into the physical, to learn not to feel trapped in the body. Your purpose is to work out this resistance, to feel as free in the body as you do when you are not in it. It is just a vehicle.*"

She continued to resist the need to return to Earth in a new body, stating that it was so easy to stay in the spirit realm, why did she have to return? The counsellors then stated:

"*So you can help others. You can't help others until you learn it yourself.*"

The counsellors continued by explaining that once she stopped resisting the human experience, she wouldn't need to experience it anymore. But she needed to experience that world sufficiently to know all the different forms of energy as part of the soul's development. She then agreed to make the return journey back to Earth.

The body is just another form of energy, and developing as a soul requires learning how to control and reorganise that energy. The likely success or failure of the life we are currently living depends to a large extent on understanding how energy works. This is explained later in the section "Thought Creates Matter".

In his 1992 work *The Tibetan Book of Living and Dying*, Sogyal Rinpoche, a Tibetan Dzogchen lama of the Nyingma tradition, explains the importance of the physical experience, and its effect on what happens when we die:

"Whatever state of mind we are in now, whatever kind of person we are now, that is what we will be like when we die, if we do not change. That is why it is so absolutely important to use this lifetime to purify our mind stream, and so our basic being and character, while we can."

The Christian faith has the same message in the Bible, which says: *Do unto others as you would have them do unto you.*

It is a way of thinking, and a way of acting. We have to learn to be good souls.

How the Soul Develops

The key to understanding how a soul develops is to firstly understand that there are *two* personalities involved during the time that the soul is on Earth: the human personality and the soul personality. These two personalities should merge during the soul's time within a human body for maximum development potential, but this is not as easy as it sounds. The merger should commence as soon as possible.

In Dr Michael Newton's book *Life Between Lives* (2009), a textbook that explains the regression of hypnotic subjects back to the spirit world, he was able to get fairly precise information about the stage of development of a soul (in other words, how advanced the soul is) through his questioning about what that soul did (if anything) during the period the soul may have been inside the mother's womb with the baby foetus. Dr Newton's questioning would ascertain when the soul first entered the womb and how long it stayed there during the pregnancy, what kind of brain the soul encountered in the foetus, how the emotional system of the foetus affected the brain, and whether the soul was finding it easy to integrate with the personality it met with in the foetus.

If the soul was able to talk easily about how it went about integrating its personality with that of the foetus/baby, it would normally indicate a more experienced or advanced soul. Resistance by a baby to the soul's integration may be because the baby's mind is heavy or dense and not quick, or perhaps because of resistance from the mother who perhaps wasn't ready for pregnancy. Conversely, a child with a quick mind has challenges for the soul because of the number of impulses and thoughts emanating from the mind and personality, which requires flexibility.

A good integration will make for an easier life, though at the time of choosing a body to enter for the soul's next life there is a certain amount of 'hit or miss' about the actual body they will encounter. This is why early integration between the baby's brain and personality and the soul's personality is essential. A young soul may not yet be sufficiently adept at integration, which will make the coming life within that body more problematic.

Once fully stabilised in the infant's body, souls quickly lose awareness of their true spiritual nature and the knowledge available to the soul in its normal (non-physical) world. This "drawing of the curtain" is designed by Source to enhance the challenge of learning through its physical journey. But souls still have the opportunity to contact "home" and obtain guidance from their support team and higher self that is still resident there, through methods such as impingement, intuition, dreams, and out-of-body experiences, as will be explained later. This way, the soul can attempt to stay on track with its planned destiny even though forces may take the soul off course.

Integration of the soul with a new body can be problematic. Dr Newton reports that when souls enter a human body on Earth, they come into dense matter because their host bodies contain primitive animal energy. Arrival can be a difficult process, far more difficult in fact than at the time of departure of the soul. In *Memories of the Afterlife*, a person was taken forwards from the interlife (when she was still in spirit form) to the time of entry into her current mother's womb, where she experienced a 'sudden jolt as her vibration lowered' to allow integration of her soul with the human embryo. The arrival and merger of the soul with the growing human requires a lowering of frequency to match that of the human.

The journey of the soul back into life is described in Dr Michael Newton's *Life Between Lives*. Hypnotherapy clients have stated that their guides accompany them a little of the way to a kind of exit portal before separating. The soul then senses that they are passing through a sort of tunnel or vortex back to Earth and the new body. Dr Newton says a client has remarked that they went "from light into darkness (the portal) and then felt the warmth of the womb".

The soul has a natural pure refined energy which does not easily blend with human hosts. It takes experience to integrate properly, and this often doesn't occur fully with younger souls where the soul and the brain of the new body are in conflict. Body energy and soul energy can be adversely affected by vibrational resonances or frequencies which are not in harmony with each other. Body and soul must smoothly coexist for humans to be productive.

It is now understood through research that we have chosen the body we are using for this life. This was done while we were still in the spirit realm. In Dr Newton's books, *Journey of Souls, Destiny of Souls,* and *Life*

Between Lives, the selection of a body the soul will inhabit for this life is described. The body review area in the spirit realm is usually visualised as round with large panels or screens that appear as transparent sheets of liquid energy. Futuristic scenes of people and events are displayed like in a theatre for the soul who is ready to enter a new life.

This concept of 'screens' where we can view our future lives is not quite as futuristic science fiction as it might seem. In Lynne McTaggart's books *The Field* and *The Intention Experiment*, she explains the quantum physics position that reality is not fixed, but fluid and open to influence. This is explained in detail from pages 47-51. In essence, subatomic particles exist in a state of potential until observed or thought about. This is science fact. As McTaggart says, if consciousness operates at the quantum frequency level, it would naturally reside outside space and time, and we should thus have access to both past and future information. If humans are able to influence quantum events, they are also able to affect events or moments other than in the present. McTaggart postulates that it may be that *our future already exists in some nebulous state that we actualise in the present.* Consequently, when we are in the body review area looking at future bodies, once we settle on a body for our next life, that body can then become real.

We are assisted in our choice of body by spirit-realm planners who help us to find the best candidate bodies to help address our strengths and weaknesses. The genes of our parents are vital as the human body we choose will have their genes, which will couple with our own soul personality. The combination represents the duality of human mind and the spirit in our bodies. The best combinations are where the body's brain and personality are complimentary to the soul's personality. For instance, a low energy, passive soul may combine best with a restless, aggressive brain to combat the timid nature of the soul. Similarly, a powerful, self-indulgent soul would need a calmer, slower body. However, in the wrong combinations, the mixture could prove to be dangerous and volatile or, alternatively, completely ineffective for learning and development. Mental distress, in Dr Newton's opinion, often derives from a poor soul-body connection.

Dr Newton states that souls inhabiting physical bodies take this responsibility very seriously, even to the extent of being inside non-functional bodies. The souls are not materially trapped. For instance, a soul may inhabit a comatose host body for many years and not abandon it until death. These souls are able to roam freely across the land visiting other souls who might be taking brief trips away from their bodies during normal sleep states. During these travels, a small portion of a soul's energy is left behind so they can return quickly if needed.

We are always linked to the spirit realm, our true home, through a cord, known as 'the silver cord' which will never become severed except at the time of actual death of the body. During astral projection and out-of-body experiences, practitioners have described this cord as a strong, silver-coloured, elastic cord which joins a person's physical body to its astral energy body. It is an assurance during dream-time travelling by the soul that the soul will not become 'disconnected' from its current physical body. Mystics have said that if a person is near to death, the astral body slowly separates itself from the physical body and the silver cord breaks, making a complete and irreversible separation of the two bodies. Practitioners at the Monroe Institute which specialised in out-of-body experiences have called this break on death a 'permanent astral projection' that cannot be undone.

Occupancy of the Human Body by a Soul

Many spiritually advanced humans have discussed the occupancy of human bodies by souls. Throughout this book, proof is offered of this reality.

In her spiritual masterpiece *Initiation*, Elizabeth Haich has said that we occupy a physical body but the immortal body is the spiritual body or being that we also occupy. This could be said to be the real 'you', your soul. Most religions agree that the spiritual body or being is an entity that is aware, creative and has a personality. However, as mentioned earlier, it is not composed of matter or of any other component of the physical world. It is an immortal unit of awareness that cannot perish but can, and does, download itself into physical matter for periods of time. It follows from this description that death is little more than a spiritual abandonment of the body the soul occupied for a while.

The 18th century mystic Emanuel Swedenborg was, like Elizabeth Haich, a spiritual adept who revealed the occupancy of human bodies by souls. He wrote about his findings in his book *Treatise Concerning Heaven and Hell* (1794), so named as the book describes the different states of mind that may be exhibited by a dead person. He appeared to be able to communicate with the dead, and was able to tell living persons intimate details that he had been given by a dead person to pass on. According to Swedenborg, man is a spirit who inhabits a body, and, at death, the man leaves his body behind and continues to exist in an incorporeal form. When the heart beat ceases, the spirit passes on to another plane of existence.

As was mentioned previously, we *chose* our bodies for this incarnation, even though our human personality may sometimes dislike what it has to work with and, thus, may find itself at odds with our soul's intentions. Our higher-self chose the body for a reason, a purpose to be experienced, and the human personality has to live with this. Unfortunately, not understanding the reason for the choice may cause us to lose self-esteem and perhaps enjoyment of our physical life. This may be a hurdle or task we set ourselves to overcome in this life.

In her many lectures, Elizabeth Kubler-Ross described the physical body as a house or temple or, as she referred to it when speaking to children, a cocoon, which our souls inhabit for a certain number of months or years until we make the transition called death. At the time of death, we shed this cocoon and are, once again, free as a butterfly. This was the symbolic language that Dr Kubler-Ross used when talking to dying children and their siblings.

C.S Lewis is quoted as saying "You don't have a soul. You are a soul. You have a body." The scientist Dr Bruce Lipton stated that our true self is not part of the body. Our true self is the soul, which is separate from the body. The film *Avatar* (2009) is a good example from Hollywood of how we download into other bodies and other worlds to experience life.

It should be remembered that almost everything that matters or affects us as we live our lives on Earth is "unseen". The soul, which is our real self, is unseen, as are thoughts, energy, air, viruses, gases, and so on.

Rudolf Steiner, in his 1922 work *Theosophy*, understood that just because something was unseen did not make it irrelevant. Indeed, he took a dim view of those who required "sight" before they would believe in the spirit world. He stated:

Only to recognise higher worlds when one has seen them is a hindrance in the way of this very seeing. The will, first of all to understand through sound thinking what can later be seen, furthers that seeing. It conjures forth important powers of the soul which lead to this seership.

We must open our minds to higher worlds.

The support team

When the soul incarnates into a physical form which the soul will inhabit during its time on Earth, the soul doesn't travel alone. The soul is supported during its occupation of the body by a support team, often referred to as spirit guides, guardians or angels, who reside in the soul's home base, but are close by, watching over us, and always at hand when needed. This home base is at another level of existence, which we can call "the spirit realm". Some people, including some progressive, open-minded scientists recently, have called it a "parallel universe". The support team is there when we need them 'in a blink of an eye'. We also have our higher self, that part of the soul's energy that was left behind in the spirit realm which can guide us from the soul level when we face difficulties in our life on Earth.

Some portion of our soul will continue to reside at the home base and, as death approaches, an increasing portion of the soul may return home, as the soul's activity and energy requirements in the physical world diminish. The energy of the soul, as reported by Dr Newton from his regressive Life-between-Life hypnotherapy sessions detailed in his book *Destiny of Souls*, is able to divide into identical parts, similar to a hologram. Because of the dual capability of all souls, part of our light energy always remains behind in the spirit realm. Thus, we can meet loved ones when we die, even though they died many years ago and have since incarnated again.

Dr Newton notes that an advanced soul may bring no more than 25% of its total energy capacity to earth. Such a soul has the ability to utilise the energy brought to Earth very effectively, whereas less advanced souls may bring up to 70% depending on the likely difficulty of the life to be embarked on. But even an advanced soul should always bring enough energy for its purpose in the coming life. The energy of a more evolved soul is refined, elastic and vigorous in small quantities, which younger souls will develop over time as the quality of their vibrational power increases with the soul's experience and wisdom, enabling them to bring smaller quantities of energy with them.

Before we embark on a new life, we are given advice on the likely energy requirements of the body to be occupied. The decision on how much energy we should take with us, and how much we leave behind in the spirit realm is left up to us. But our life is harder on earth if we take too little energy, and we cannot go back and take more after incarnating, as this affects the delicate balance between the human body and the soul. If our lives are likely to involve trauma or testing circumstances, we should have sufficient energy reserves to cope with this. Souls tend to want to leave as much as possible of their energy behind as they love their home and what they do there. Sometimes, for karmic-learning reasons, a soul who has long-term aggressive tendencies may agree to limit the energy taken for a forthcoming life, reducing the ability to be violent, which represents an important step forwards as a learning experience to change the character of that soul. In Dr Newton's *Memories of the Afterlife* (2009), one of his subjects had incarnated as a lady with no use of her legs as a learning experience after many lives of committing violent acts.

One of the things the soul is learning about is "physicality" – the experience of living inside a human body and the sensations allowed through that reality. That is a key reason why the soul incarnated into the body it now inhabits: to learn, experience, experiment and gather knowledge. Living on Earth is a difficult experience, but learning can be accelerated when things do not go smoothly. For most people, problems are a daily occurrence requiring resolution and solutions.

Certain souls incarnate for other specific reasons, such as to help humans in specific ways or advance technology. But learning, gaining experience and knowledge are what the soul takes back "home" at the end of the physical body's life. This is how the soul develops.

The soul will always have a designated life path that it is meant to pursue during each incarnation into physical form, and this should not be greatly deviated from if at all possible. We know what our life path is if we focus on it. Unfortunately, it is not always possible to follow that path as will be shown.

The soul has a communication channel with its support team and with its "oversoul" which is meant to be clear and unobstructed at all times. However, living in the physical world can compromise the integrity of that connection. As an aside, our closest friends are part of our "oversoul". From Source, large groups of souls are formed, which then form smaller groups of "oversouls" which comprise usually around twelve individual souls, who incarnate from time to time into the physical realm, interacting with each other across countless lives to assist the development of each other's souls. These members of the "oversoul" may spend short or long periods of time with each other across incarnations depending on the role they have agreed to play in each soul's planned development. There is also a wider cluster of thousands of souls that interact with us from life to life to assist our development.

The prime motivation of souls is to move towards a greater goodness and back to a merger with the Source that created us. Advanced subjects of Dr Newton talk about the time of merger when they will join a sphere of dense purple light with the all-knowing Presence. The closest we come over thousands of incarnations until this time of release is when we meet our "Council of Elders" who conduct a life review at the end of our lives. Here we can experience true divine knowledge briefly. The deep sadness we often feel in moments of contemplation is the desire to reunite with our friends in the spirit realm, and ultimately to reunite with the Source of our existence.

Dr Newton states that the Council is looking to see if the inner immortal character of our soul maintained its integrity in terms of values, ideals and action during incarnation. The Council want to know if our soul was overwhelmed or sabotaged by our host body, or if we 'shined through'. Did our soul effectively merge as a partner to the human brain as one harmonious outward human personality? How did we deal with problems we faced, did we pick ourselves up after failure? How was our conduct towards others, towards power and dominance over others, and so forth?

Behavioural conduct is of paramount importance to the Council of Elders and this denotes how we are spiritually progressing. Being encased in a human body whose brain is primarily concerned with the body's own survival can cause morality and ethical issues for the soul. Dr Newton states, towards the end of *Destiny of Souls*, that in the search for our path of spirituality it is wise to ask oneself "what sort of behavioural code do I believe in?" He says that whether or not we have any religious associations during our life is not relevant as we are evaluated after death *solely on our conduct and values.*

Dr Newton's sessions show that most of us start our new incarnations by making lots of silly mistakes and taking wrong turns, accepting temptations and so on, but by the end of that life we have become wiser. He says:

"The idea of coming back in repeated incarnations is that eventually we will get it right early on and lead productive lives from the beginning. In this quest we are often ego-driven and we forget that what is good for us is generally good for other people. The solution for all

of us to improve is staying with the process of continuing evolution to become better than we are. We are given many host bodies and all of them are imperfect. Rather than being obsessive about a body which will last only one lifetime, concentrate on the evolution of your soul Self and rely on your spiritual power. On the road of life we must take responsibility for all our decisions without blaming other people for life's setbacks that bring unhappiness."

The soul's memories of past lives (and the soul's memory of existence between lives) are generally not able to be recalled by a soul returning to earth in a new body, and so the past cannot be utilised to assist development. This is not necessarily a bad thing, as releasing the past is a vital function in a soul's development (see the later Section, "Letting Go"). In any event, the soul's advancing personality and behavioural conduct should naturally flow through even if the past/between-life memories do not.

From the time of first creation, the intention is that the soul should develop in accordance with the original blueprint. However, as the soul grows and develops through its stages (infant, baby, young, mature, old), the soul will be affected by multiple influences due to it being housed in a porous body. Correct development requires a continuous connection back to the source of creation and this is not always possible.

A critical question when considering the development of the soul is: Who should have ownership, possession and control of a human body? Is the human body the exclusive domain of the soul? Should the human body be the exclusive domain of the soul? Based on the law of free will, and the concept of 'sovereign right' over a body and, above all, the need for that soul to have the best chance to spiritually develop through the experience gained while occupying a physical body, the answer must be "yes" - that each human body should be the exclusive domain of the designated soul.

Not all human bodies contain souls, although if a body was designated as a vehicle to be used by a particular soul, it should never be forced to share the body, or worse, be 'displaced' or shunted out of the body. The soul should always be owner, possessor and controller of the body until such time as it chooses freely to leave the body, or to freely invite other spirits or entities to join it. The mystic Rudolf Steiner, amongst many other mystics across the years, viewed the human body as a spiritual vessel, open to occupation by other forces, spirits and entities. A film which depicts very well this process of 'shunting out the possessor of a body' is *Being John Malkovich* (1999).

The transhumanist agenda, under which human beings will be implanted with a radio-frequency identity chip, merging the human with artificial intelligence, would effectively displace the soul as the primary possessor of a human body. This is not desirable as it would impede development of the soul's integration with the human host. This is because the human body's thoughts and actions would be controlled by others, whose motives are unknown, and are unlikely to be beneficial, or in line with the soul's plan for this life. The soul's spiritual development would certainly be impeded. Details of the transhumanist agenda are covered in Appendix 4.

Similarly, the idea of 'storing' one's soul and temporarily replacing it with someone else's so that the human body can perceive or feel the world differently by experiencing someone else's soul and consciousness, and creating different conduct for the body the soul now inhabits, is not desirable and is poignantly dealt with in the film *Cold Souls* (2010). The process of soul transfer is discussed in Part 2.

The soul is the intended inhabitant of the physical human body, so that it can grow spiritually while in the physical plane of existence. The body is simply the vehicle used by the soul so that it can experience another environment other than its home (non-physical) base - in this case, the three dimensional (physical) environment called Earth. There are also many other dimensions, environments and planetary systems around the universe which offer different experiences as the soul develops.

From Barham & Greene's pioneering work *The Silver Cord*, and from Dr Michael Newton's *Destiny of Souls*, it can be concluded that souls are created from a pure, benevolent source, and are therefore not evil. As souls go through their lives, because they derive from Source, they are endowed with a facet of divinity. We carry that source with us at all times. However, almost all souls while inhabiting human bodies have to work with bodies which are not as pure as the soul, and may have been corrupted or tampered with to some extent.

This is because the human body, which houses the soul during the life of the body, is not created from a pure, benevolent source and has few defence mechanisms built in to repel predators. The human brain, for instance, has no firewall. This allows tampering by those with knowledge of how to control the human body. This can also hamper the speed of development of the soul from the time of its birth. The source for the creation of the human body is of extraterrestrial origin, as detailed extensively in the author's book *They Exist*.

The energy field of the human body is an outer layer of energy that emanates from every person. Physicians who study the body's energy fields have stated the etheric body is a holographic energy template that can show the state of health or illness of a physical body. Illness appears in this template long before it appears in the physical body. Thoughts and events influence the state of the energy template/body in positive or negative ways. Cuts and holes (energetic openings) develop in the energy body, also known as the aura, in various ways. Where extreme trauma is involved, a part ('fragment') of the soul may separate from the physical body in order to avoid the pain and trauma of the experience.

When a soul fragments, it creates a hole within the energy body, allowing the potential arrival of unseen forms or entities which "join" the soul within the physical body. Spiritual healers can see holes in this etheric field, which they say looks like a torn curtain. The fragmented parts of the soul can be retrieved, which will create an energetic barrier around the energy body, sealing and protecting the energy body from unwanted spirits, who may change our behavioural conduct, getting into it. Specific events such as emotional or sexual abuse during childhood, fear, terror, bullying, control and dominance by others, addictions, excessive use of drugs or alcohol, sharing or mingling of body fluids, loss or death of loved ones, traumatic accidents or exposure to traumatic events can cause soul loss, damage the energy body, and lower body frequency.

In case uninvited entities diminish the soul's ability to communicate with its support team, which we may not appreciate has happened, we should always be aware of the many methods by which our support team in the spirit realm contacts *us*. It doesn't always have to be *us* contacting our support team, they can intervene if we are going way off our life plan, even if we don't ask. The usual way we are contacted is by receipt of "messages" in a variety of ways that have meaning to the individual for whom the message is designed. We should always be sufficiently alert and aware to be able to receive these messages that arrive at important moments, (known as "synchronicity"). Our guides and support team can find amazing ways to contact us if we open our eyes and minds and allow ourselves to be divinely contacted. We are not alone.

An unseen world

David Icke points out in *Infinite Love is the Only Truth – Everything Else is Illusion* that the unseen world, which is another dimension of reality, sometimes called the spirit world or realm, vibrates at a speed too fast for us to see. We can only see 'luminous matter', which reflects electromagnetic light, but 95% or more of the mass of the universe is known as 'dark matter' which doesn't reflect light and so cannot be seen (the film *Dark Matter* (2007) gives a good explanation of the importance of dark matter in the universe). Indeed, Icke reports that the electromagnetic spectrum is only 0.005 percent of the estimated mass of the universe and human sight can only see a minute fraction even of these electromagnetic frequencies, as we can only see 'visible light'.

With this knowledge of our visible limits, it makes a mockery of the scientific view that there are no other forms of life in the universe. How would 'almost-blind' humans really know anything about the rest of the universe? Other alien forms may well operate in realms unseen by the human eye. If such 'alien forms' are ever sighted by humans, it is simply because they entered the frequency range of humans. And when they are no longer visible, it is because they have left our visible frequency range. An important non-human spirit dimension, which regularly interacts with the human dimension, is revealed in Appendix 2, although it should be noted that this dimension is not the dimension that the soul returns to on the death of the human body hosting the soul.

Healing

Whatever happens during a soul's time within a human body, however traumatic events may be, on arrival back in the spirit realm the soul is fully healed, and purified with unconditional love, and made ready for its next adventure.

Rudolf Steiner, who was a spiritual celebrity at the start of the 20th century, called the energy field around the body an 'etheric body' which interpenetrates the physical body. Steiner stated that all the physical organs are maintained in their form and shape by the currents and movements of the etheric body. Steiner went on to add that the human also has an astral body which is the link to the spirit realm, and this is where consciousness derives from. This remains with, and is an integral part of, the soul after death.

It is through sickness within the etheric body that the physical body gets sick. As Anita Moorjani has said following her health-restoring near-death experience (see *Dying To Be Me*, reviewed later), a healthy etheric body ensures the physical body will follow. A century before Steiner, mystics such as Emanuel Swedenborg, Dr James Graham, William Blake, Franz Mesmer and Dr John Mainaduc were saying the same thing concerning the importance of the etheric or energy body in directing our health, vitality and happiness.

Soul Learning and Development

In 1968, Martha Barham and James Greene published a detailed treatise on soul development, entitled *The Silver Cord: Lifeline to the Unobstructed*. Barham & Greene's book is an excellent introduction to the creation of souls, the non-physical world of our souls after death, and why our souls return in new physical bodies to continue developing. The information was gleaned through 'dark-room sessions' with disincarnates who *actually materialised* for periods of time from other planes of existence to impart wisdom about the life beyond. These materialised entities were called "guides" or "spirits" by Barham & Greene. The teachings are persuasive.

The Soul

The guides or spirits that materialised and are referenced in *The Silver Cord* stated that each of us has a soul, a spiritual aspect every bit as real as our physical aspect. This is confirmed by multiple sources during the course of this book.

Souls are created by God, also referred to as Source, or Source of All Divinity, and souls are tiny facets *of* Source. Unlike our physical aspect, the soul never dies;

once given birth (from Source), it lives forever. Each soul has a purpose and evolves before finally merging back into Source to enhance Source, contributing to the evolutionary growth of Source.

Similar to Barham & Greene's magnificent work, in 2005 Rosalind McKnight published a book entitled *Soul Journeys* which details almost equivalent information. McKnight's information was accessed from her higher self, which she called "Radiant Lady", and which she said appeared to her, dictating information to her about the afterlife of the soul. Neil Donald Walsch did something similar with his series of excellent books entitled *Conversations With God*. As Rosalind McKnight put it in *Soul Journeys*, how do we find out what the next world is like? Simple: Ask someone who lives there and record what is said. This is what Barham & Greene also did, enabling them to write down precise information about the spirit realms.

McKnight states that we live in our soul bodies until such time as we evolve to the highest spiritual dimension – when the soul body is dissolved and our spiritual body of pure light resides in the presence of the Godhead. Essentially, we evolve through different levels until we are back in the presence of God, where we first started. The core of McKnight's book *Soul Journeys* is that the purpose for being on Earth is to learn, grow, live and love through the real energy, the spirit, and not be attached to and controlled by the physical.

Returning to Barham & Greene's work, the guides or spirits referenced in *The Silver Cord* tell us that, upon birth from Source, the soul enters a non-physical, spirit realm that they call "the unobstructed world". While there, souls do not carry the shape of a physical body but exist as patterns of energy. As with information received from regressive hypnosis sources (such as Dr Michael Newton's *Journey of Souls* and Karen Joy's *Other Lives, Other Realms*), the guides here state that we select our planned incarnation on Earth to maximise our learning while in a physical body. They call the planning of a future life "the government of life"; however, this can be adversely affected by many unplanned factors, which they refer to as the "gamble of life". Adverse, unexpected events may end up limiting our learning or even the amount of time spent in a particular physical body.

They state that the soul will enter a physical body about the time that the infant takes its first breath on its own. However, in Dr Newton's book *Destiny of Souls*, he states that some (more advanced) souls download/arrive during the later development of the foetus, rather than at actual birth, as the calibration between the soul's personality and the human personality and brain may be problematic, making earlier calibration and balancing desirable. When entering the body, the soul goes through a process of solidifying in the body, calibrating itself with the personality features of the infant. Throughout life, there tend to be struggles between the mind or higher self of the soul, and the human personality and its physical body.

After death of the physical body, our souls leave the body and the physical environment we have lived in (that the guides call "the *obstructed* world") and return to the *unobstructed* world from which we originated. The soul will undergo a series of re-orientating processes, such as meeting soul mates, guides and other entities. Spirit guides from the 'unobstructed world' assist on arrival (in a more 'hands on' way, but similar to the role they have in assisting us while we are in a physical body).

While on Earth the guides participate through activities such as 'impingement' where a soul is nudged or urged in one way or another to take a certain direction – essentially, a psychic nudge to pay attention to certain thoughts, urges, dreams, wishes or hunches. Free will cannot be impinged though. The concept of 'impingement' to keep a person following their 'life plan' was the basis of the 2011 film *The Adjustment Bureau.*

Once created it is impossible for a soul not to return to Source at the end of its learning experiences. To ensure this, Source created a fail-safe design, called "reincarnation", which is explained below. Source itself is an impenetrable field of energy that souls are not permitted to enter until they have completed their destiny.

Rarely does a soul complete all its learning in one incarnation. This necessitates a need for 'reincarnation'. The same process will occur again as happened before. In particular, the soul will attempt to gain the experiences it needs to evolve. Reincarnation is a *fail-safe design of Source* when events get in the way of planned experiences of a soul. The soul will get as many opportunities for learning as it needs.

Reference is made in Barham & Greene's work to Arthur Young's book, *The Reflexive Universe*, where he states

"If the soul is immortal, why then is a body mortal? It is because only the finite (or mortal) body is appropriate for learning. If the body were indestructible, it could not be injured and no learning could occur. This is the reason for mortality....it is only by

taking roles that the self learns to act, to achieve the competence required in order to have dominion over nature, to become, as Genesis puts it, 'as wise as gods, knowing good from evil'."

The Soul's need for physical living

The key to living, as we are told by the 'guides' who communicated with Barham and Greene and others in the 'dark room sessions', is to focus on "acquiring experiences we can only have while in a physical body", and the guides discouraged focus on the more esoteric aspects of spirituality such as sitting in silence or monastic isolation from living.

They state:

"To spend too much time seeking escape from the challenges of physical life with its many frustrations will, ultimately, slow down our spiritual progression."

There is a lot of time for non-physical spiritual progression while not in a physical body.

Learning, experiencing, observing, developing from *living* is essential - *not* running away from life. Living is the way we advance spiritually. The problem is that in living in today's world we have lost a lot of the balance of life from days gone by when there was less greed, less competitiveness, more sharing and caring, and more awareness of our spiritual nature.

Consequently, more sensitive souls have a tendency to shy away from living once that soul realises what is involved in the jungle we enter. Much of living is unpleasant and highly stressed and was perhaps not anticipated when they incarnated. But the only way to develop, to grow spiritually, is to *experience*. The guides state that completing our goals in the physical world is the most difficult step on the road to 'returning to Source' which they say is a seven-step process, the first and most important of which is completion of the physical living experience.

Soul Mates

The interesting thing that the guides state is that we are never born alone from Source. Other souls, known as soul mates, are created with us (in a small group of usually twelve souls known as 'the oversoul', which was mentioned earlier). This is a beautiful design to make the journey from Source and ultimately back to Source more enjoyable and stable. They are almost like marker buoys along the way whom we meet regularly across the course of our many lives. They can help with the 'gamble of life' where planned events do not work out, such as where chosen parents turn out differently from the way we anticipated. People such as chosen parents are often not part of our own inner soul group, but are part of a larger cluster of thousands of souls we associate with in the spirit realms, who have come to play a role in our spiritual development.

Parenting

The early learning experiences of a new infant possessing a soul are considered extremely important. At birth, aside from having a sexual identification, physical characteristics, and a basic configuration of potential personality traits, for all practical purposes the infant is a vulnerable new being ready for fresh learning.

As infants and young children, we are literally at the mercy of our parents. Initially, we need nourishment, physical care, protection and security. Then we need guidance for physical skill development. Our first few years of contact with our family contribute heavily to our basic attitudinal and emotional programming/conditioning. The basic attitudes towards life we acquire as children influence our behaviour through our lives. Forcing children into a pre-determined mould is deplored by the materialised spirit entities that Barham and Greene interacted with. They urge parents to support the uniqueness of each child's personality traits, abilities, interests and so on; otherwise, immense damage can be done - damage which affects the usefulness and development of that life, and perhaps even future lives (as practitioners of regressive hypnosis/therapy have reported).

The Life Plan

How do we stay in touch with our destiny for this life?

How can we avoid being hopelessly diverted by living and fail to meet our desired goals?

Before we are born, we devise a pre-birth 'government of life' plan which is the template we use during our life on Earth. We have two sources of guidance. We have guides (the people interested in us) and also our own wisdom (called intuition). However, our plans can be affected by sheer chance, accident, unexpected life changes, the unpredictability of others, or bad luck, all of which are called the 'gamble of life'. This is one of the many ways to learn devised by Source. Prayer and meditation can assist our ability to stay in touch with our guides, the spirit realm and Source. We can ask for help.

We also continue to communicate with the 'unobstructed' (the non-physical world) through our out-of-body experiences (OBEs) while asleep. This is where our spiritual essence literally leaves the physical body and travels to the spirit realm to communicate with our friends as energy patterns.

Normally, we cannot recall leaving our physical body during sleep, but some practitioners of OBEs can look down and see their sleeping body lying on the bed. They can describe their re-entry into the empty shell after their journey. They often describe seeing the silver cord that connects the spirit to the body. Sometimes, they describe a tugging sensation of the cord pulling them back if they have been away too long.

During an out-of-body experience, the soul usually first assumes an ethereal form resembling our physical form. It may change that form to its original energy pattern when communicating directly with the spirit realm. Out-of-body experiences are a natural design for nurturing, as we are a prisoner in our physical body and need to leave it sometimes. There are no learning techniques required to leave the body during sleep. However, it is *impossible* for a soul not to return to the body immediately if there is any significant physical threat to the body. This is achieved through the existence of the *silver cord* which always ties us to our bodies.

The approach of death of the physical body

Shortly before death, especially where in coma, extreme pain or lingering illness, the soul will begin to be freer to come and go, to leave the body, and return to the body. This helps with the acceptance of death. The silver cord ensures we cannot leave the body permanently before physical death. We are always in our body when it dies (although in deaths where there is trauma or severe pain, the soul may exit just before bodily death).

The transition of the soul after physical death is a gradual one. The guides state that it takes several hours, or even days, to feel fully acclimated back to the 'unobstructed'.

There are three stages of death. Firstly, there is etherealisation, when the soul (spiritual energy) is released from the body but remains in a form resembling the physical body we left behind. Depending on our experience of this stage, we will move on from seconds to hours later into a pure energy form. Finally, we sever the silver cord and our connection to the physical world.

Merger back with Source

When we have finished our learning in the physical and our tasks in the non-physical ('unobstructed') world, we are ready to merge back with God, the Source.

As Richard Matheson says in *What Dreams May Come*:

"*Not everyone is reborn. Some souls are so advanced they no longer reincarnate but pass on to a level of existence beyond anything that Earth can offer, achieving a final reunion with God.*

These souls, having found no remaining lack in their attempts to atone for misdeeds or acquire knowledge, elect to join the Creator and are drawn into a state of perfect oneness with Him, becoming, as it were, integral with the universal pattern".

The Ego versus The Soul

As Eckhart Tolle said in his 1997 classic *The Power of Now*, we cannot be at ease if the ego part of our mind is running our lives, desiring that people see us in a particular way, rather than our true self.

Ego identifies with things that are not 'us', such as possessions, social status and recognition, physical appearance, personal and family history and so on. Death is the stripping away of all that is not 'us'. So, sooner or later, we will have to relinquish those things that the ego identifies with. Consequently, to get more of what we desire in life, we need to listen to the guidance of our higher self, our soul source, rather than our ego.

The ego has a limited view of the world; whereas, the soul can see the wider picture concerning actions we take, healing and spiritual development. The two views are entirely incompatible. The ego only identifies with the body and its personality and does not know how others will be affected by its choices in a wider context of development. It knows nothing about the soul's wider vision for spiritual development and learning. Essentially, our human personality and ego, our conscious mind, is very limited in its understanding and does not know the full picture. So to base long-term decision-making on what the ego demands has to be wrong.

Guidance from our soul source comes through intuition. Yet, it is very easy to rationalise away any message which comes to us intuitively. There are many reasons for this, but a crucial one is our early conditioning and our daily social conditioning, which limit our soul's vision. This vision should be a vision of service to others rather than the ego's vision of service to self. We can access this vision the more we listen to our intuition.

Accessing this vision may, over time, cause our interests, priorities and goals to shift, perhaps even reducing our material possessions and worldly achievements. The body's ego may not, however, appreciate such changes in "status". It may be that change can only come when a catalyst for change occurs, a life crisis, such as divorce, illness, financial loss, death of someone close to you, or a natural life transition occurs, such as reaching of major life milestones which then give us the time and space to focus on deeper questions of purpose. Then we can stop the treadmill of life for a while and ask ourselves questions, including: Who am I? What am I doing here? What is my life's purpose?

Only when we reach what Susan Wisehart calls "the soul-infused personality" will real change occur. We will stop wanting something back for what we give; we will stop 'keeping score' of the hours of service given or the amount of money we contribute, all the while considering ourselves superior to those around us. We will have a genuine heart-felt desire to serve and help, a genuine feeling of unconditional giving and love. The need for someone else's approval or recognition will disappear. Our own spiritual growth, which is the true agenda of the soul, will then become obvious.

Wisehart, the author of *Soul Visioning*, says many of her clients feel they have failed in life because they didn't accomplish anything 'great' or fulfil some grand life purpose. She reminds them that one's greatest purpose is to experience wholeness as a spiritual being, and to express love every day, whether by extending kindness and patience when waiting in line at the grocery store, being peaceful in a traffic jam, or practicing forgiveness of oneself or others.

Wisehart, who is a certified hypnotherapist with over thirty years of experience, and is also certified through Dr Michael Newton in life-between-lives regression, is a leader in the field of integration of the soul personality with that of the human body/ego. This key area of healing is rarely discussed beyond Newton Institute practitioners of regressive hypnotherapy; yet, it is one of the most powerful areas of analysis for diagnosing mental distress.

The separate existences of the soul and the ego are acknowledged within Islamic mysticism. A major feature of Sufi practitioners involves the breaking down of the 'false self', the ego. Sufism teaches that what we generally imagine to be our own self, the ego, is really not us at all, and operates independently of us, and is made up of negative traits such as envy, pride, jealousy, false attachments. The breaking down of the 'false self' allows the unveiling of the true self, the soul. Similarly, the important Gnostic text, the *Pistis Sophia*, clearly references the coming together of the soul and ego within the human body, the soul 'descending' from higher realms into the body.

As Susan Wisehart says:

"When we stand at the top of the mountain, our view is vaster than if we stand at the bottom, when we can only see what is right in front of us. From the spirit realm, we can see the bigger picture.

When we forget this, we become so mired in the dense physical dimension that we believe that all we are is a body that gets sick, dies, and is forever gone. Reminded of who we really are, we often become less identified with our everyday ego persona."

Letting Go

The speed at which the soul can develop is inhibited until we learn to let go of the past and attachments that hold us back. It will be said many times during the course of this book that, on death, we should relax and let go. This can be done in a split-second, but we must relinquish in our minds all attachments - whether to our family, our house, our possessions, our past history and, of course, our body.

The process of releasing physical, material, attachments on death is easier *if we address this state during life.*

In *A New Earth*, Eckhart Tolle retells the parable of the two Zen monks, Tanzan and Ekido, who were walking along a muddy road when they came upon a young woman who was trying to cross the road, but the mud was so deep that it would have ruined the silk kimono she was wearing. Tanzan picked her up and carried her to the other side. The monks then walked on in silence. Five hours later, as they were approaching their lodgings temple, Ekido couldn't restrain himself any longer. "Why did you carry that girl across the road?" he asked. "We monks are not supposed to do things like that". Tanzan replied: "I put the girl down hours ago. Are you still carrying her?"

This is a fine illustration of the inability or unwillingness of the human mind to let go of the past.

Most people continually accumulate baggage from the past which they carry around with them. What a heavy burden this is for the mind, and it is the source of many people's problems in life.

When an emotion appears, if we don't let it go, the problem we bury will run our lives. Michael Singer comments, in his 2007 book *The Untethered Soul*, that once we face our disturbances, we realise that there is a layer of pain seated deep in the core of our hearts. This pain is so uncomfortable, so destructive to the individual self that we spend our entire lives avoiding it. In fact, our personality develops around avoiding this pain.

Singer says that we can solve this problem by acknowledging this pain, and then relaxing and giving it the space it needs to release and burn through us. When we pass beyond this layer of pain, we will become finally free from the binds of the psyche. Letting go cleanses the heart. Life's events are not to be resisted. They are going to happen anyway. Resisting what has already happened is a waste of energy.

Ari Kopel, in *Getting Back to Source (2015)*, expresses the belief that our willingness to let go is a major part of our ability to connect directly with Source. Letting go means we are not to attach to anything in this realm. Indeed, we need to understand that we do not even originate from this plane of existence.

Letting go means letting go of physical objects and also the outcome of events, and letting go of jobs, relationships, and friendships that no longer serve us. It also means releasing circumstances in our lives that do not allow us to progress in our missions or attain a healthy body or a higher spiritual level.

We need our physical body in order to operate effectively in the world and, if something such as a job or relationship is impeding us from being at peace, stressing us out, or causing ill health, we should let it go.

Learning to forgive is an important part of our soul growth. Forgiveness is simply the process of leaving the past behind, closing the door on past wrongs, mistakes, trauma. This doesn't mean we open the door again to someone who has wronged us. There is no need to allow oneself to be harmed again by doing so. Forgiving means that we no longer carry the past with us as a weight or burden.

Thought Creates Matter: The Scientific Proof of the Existence of the Soul

We are taught that consciousness came out of a material world. In reality, consciousness existed long before materialism. The late Dr Masaru Emoto wrote a masterpiece giving scientific proof of the effect of consciousness and the unseen world on our physical lives. This book is entitled *The Hidden Messages in Water* (2001). He discovered that the molecular structure of water is affected by our thoughts, words and feelings.

His discoveries about water started with the idea of freezing water and photographing the water at the exact moment that crystals formed as the water froze. He discovered that the shapes of the crystals that formed were, astonishingly, affected by our thoughts, words and intentions (feelings). For instance, the words "thank you" formed beautiful hexagonal crystals, whereas water exposed to the word "fool" produced malformed and fragmented crystals. Worse than this, water that was ignored hardly produced any form of crystal at all. From this he was able to deduce that the vibration produced by good words has a positive effect on our world, whereas the vibration produced by negative words has the opposite effect. Being ignored is the worst of all worlds. The most beautiful crystal though was produced by the *combination* of the words "love and gratitude".

As Dr Emoto puts it, "existence is vibration". He says that if we could reduce our bodies to a microscopic size, we would discover we consist of nothing more than atoms, each atom being a nucleus with electrons rotating around it. The number and shape of these electrons and their orbits gives everything a particular set of vibrational frequencies. Nothing is solid, just a nucleus surrounded by an endlessly rotating wave. Everything is moving and vibrating constantly at incredible speeds. Human beings vibrate just like everything else, and each individual vibrates at a unique frequency. We all have the sensory skills to feel the vibrations of others, which is why we feel happy in the company of some people and not with others. Attraction is caused by two humans resonating at similar energy frequencies.

Thus, if we are surrounded by love and gratitude, the molecular structure of the water flowing through our bodies will cause us to feel happy and healthy, whilst being surrounded by people who dislike us, or ignore us, will cause our bodies to become sick. As Dr Emoto concludes, water, which is so sensitive to the unique frequencies being emitted by the world, essentially and efficiently mirrors the outside world.

Lynne McTaggart takes the science behind what Dr Emoto says a stage further in her books *The Field* (2001) and *The Intention Experiment* (2007). This resulted in the conclusion, scientifically proven, that our thoughts actually create our reality.

In *The Field,* she discusses the work of a band of frontier scientists who had spent many years re-examining quantum physics and certain equations which conventional scientists had considered superfluous.

These equations, which related to something called the Zero Point Field, concerned the quantum field generated by the endless passing back and forth of energy between all subatomic particles, which never stay completely at rest, even at temperatures low enough that nothing should still move.

McTaggart states that the existence of this Field implies that all matter in the universe is connected on the subatomic level through a constant dance of quantum energy exchange. This includes human beings who can be described as packets of pulsating energy constantly interacting with this vast sea of energy in the universe. Energy is what underpins our universe.

Energy is all there is

There aren't two fundamental physical entities, one material and one immaterial; there is only one: energy. Hal Puthoff, a leader in the field of quantum physics whose work is discussed at length in *The Field*, states that if we pulled the plug on zero-point energy, all atomic structure would collapse.

Through years of well-designed experiments (explained in *The Field)*, scientists deduced that consciousness (which is an integral part of the soul) is a substance outside the confines of our bodies, and is a highly-ordered energy with the capacity to change physical matter. The scientific evidence amassed in *The*

Field suggests that directed thought has a central participatory role in creating reality. Targeted thoughts, often described as 'intention' by scientists, *appear to produce an energy potent enough to change physical reality*. The experiments made it clear that thoughts and intentions are capable of affecting everything from the simplest machines to the most complex living beings, and are an actual physical 'something' with the power to change our world. To create matter, particles simply accelerate which causes them to stick together and form concentrated energy, which we call matter.

Until these new revelations from the world of quantum physics, Newton's laws of motion and gravity had governed physics, based on the idea that matter was considered inviolate and self-contained, with its own fixed boundaries, and to change physical matter required a force or collision. Quantum physics changed all that. What the quantum physicists discovered is that every subatomic particle is not a solid and stable thing, but exists simply as a potential of any one of its future selves, in a constant state of becoming, a 'superposition', like a person staring at himself in a hall of mirrors. At the quantum level, *reality resembles unset jelly*. Matter, at its most fundamental, could not be divided into independent existing units. Things had no meaning in isolation, but only in relationship with everything else. The universe was a web of dynamic interrelationship. Matter and consciousness cannot be disassociated. It was only when scientists started to observe a subatomic particle (by taking a measurement) that the subatomic particle, that existed as 'pure potential', in a state of becoming, would 'collapse' into one particular state.

This meant that *living consciousness was the influence that turned the possibility of something into something real. We help matter to determine its final state.*

One can conclude that the most essential ingredient in creating our universe is the consciousness that observes it. In other words, nothing in the universe exists as an actual 'thing' independently of our perception of it. This leads to the amazing conclusion that *reality is not fixed, but fluid, and open to influence.*

As time progressed and scientists gathered more information through their experiments, they discovered the theory of 'entanglement', that all matter was interconnected, and potentially entangled throughout the cosmos through quantum waves. Thus, if we and all of empty space are a mass of entanglement, we must be establishing invisible connections with things at a distance to ourselves. This is why the power of thought can be picked up by someone many miles away.

Human beings have been discovered to be both receivers and transmitters of quantum wave signals. Lynne McTaggart states in *The Intention Experiment* that at least 40 top scientists in academic centres of research around the world have demonstrated that an information transfer constantly carries on between living things, and thought forms are one aspect of transmitted energy. Thoughts are clearly capable of profoundly affecting all aspects of our lives. Thoughts have a fundamental effect on us.

Lynne McTaggart also discusses the work of noetic scientists in her books. She calls these scientists 'frontier' scientists. Dan Brown brought the subject of noetic science to prominence through his excellent 2009 thriller *The Lost Symbol*. Noetic science focuses on the untapped potential of the human mind, and includes the concept that *thought* has 'mass' just like physical things. So if thought is an actual *thing*, a measurable mass and measurable entity, then it must have gravity just like physical things, enabling it to *pull things towards it*. So, in theory, we could change the world if enough people had the same thought, as 'mass thought' has a big gravitational pull, enabling actual physical change to occur.

The concept that 'thought creates' is also a key point made by Jonathan Black in his well-researched book on secret societies, *The Secret History of the World*, published in 2007. In this book, Black discusses the secret societies that have passed down to their initiates the true meaning of life, and Black summarises much of what key esoteric figures across history passed down to initiates. He says that the real secret is that *mind preceded matter*. Before the big bang there was nothing, no objects in space, no time. It was *thought* that generated physical events, which all started from the "point of singularity". And as the secret societies understand all too well, *thought* continues to be the key to creation and existence. For those who want to rule the world, therefore, thought must be contained, manipulated and controlled.

However much they might ridicule studies into non-material concepts, consciousness is relevant to even conventional scientists, as the quantum physicist Eugene Wignor has indicated. He stated that "it is not possible to formulate the laws of quantum mechanics in a fully consistent way without reference to consciousness". This is because, according to many who work in the field of quantum mechanics, including the founding father of the subject, Max Planck, consciousness is the backbone of physical material matter, not the other way round. This is clearly expounded in Lynne McTaggart's books, which are readable and explanatory, even for non-scientists.

Robert Monroe, who brought the existence of out-of-body experiences (OBEs) to public knowledge, said our souls sometimes split such that we co-exist on earth *and in other places*, a fact he was able to surmise from his OBEs. It should be noted that many spiritual healers have said that a soul will never entirely download into a human mind-body unit and entirely reside in that body. Some part continues to reside in the spirit realm, linking the two worlds. The part of the soul residing in the body-mind unit needs to have some interaction with that part located in its 'home base' and to free itself from the limiting constriction of the human physical body. Some have called this 'home base' a "parallel universe".

As reported in his 1981 survey, George Gallup Jr stated in his book *Adventures in Immortality*:

"A growing number of researchers have been gathering and evaluating the accounts of those who have had strange near-death encounters, and the preliminary results have been highly suggestive of some sort of encounter with an extra-dimensional realm of reality. Our own extensive survey is the latest in these studies and is also uncovering some trends that point toward a super parallel universe of some sort".

This is backed up by Dr Stuart Hameroff, director for the Centre for Consciousness Studies at the University of Arizona. Dr Hameroff believes that consciousness continues to exist after death in a parallel universe, and is a non-localised phenomenon which resides in the brain's microtubular structure while a person is alive and provides the link between the brain and the soul. Hameroff explains that when the body dies, the microtubules lose their quantum state, but the quantum information within the microtubules is not destroyed, it just redistributes and dissipates to the universe at large. This quantum information, our consciousness, can exist in this state independent of the body, and moves to a body residing in a parallel universe. This makes sense when considering communications with the dead, such as when a person undergoes an NDE, where the dead person says they are alright where they are. This is because they are *not actually dead* but merely existing at this point in time in a 'parallel universe'.

If we need *scientific* proof to persuade us of the existence of a soul (or consciousness) beyond our earthly existence, the evidence referenced above is where we must look. But we can experience such knowledge without being a scientist. For those who have had near-death experiences, proof of life beyond physical death is no longer required. They *know*.

PART 2:

THE TRANSFER OF SOULS AND MEMORIES FROM BODY TO BODY

The Process of Transfer

The soul is normally transferred from the current human body it occupies, once that body has died, to another human body only after the soul is back in the spirit realm and has had a period of time recalibrating and healing back there. The arrival of the soul into a new foetus and the process of soul transfer is discussed in this section and also referenced elsewhere (see Index). The process of actual death of the current human body and the arrival of the soul back into the spirit realm is discussed in later sections.

The problem with which the soul is faced is that the body containers that are used to house the soul while the soul is on Earth do not last long enough to allow sufficient time for consciousness to fully develop and mature. The maximum time frame for existence of a human body is between 80 and 100 years, and many do not last even that long as the human body has limited ability to fight disease and unforeseen accidents. Further, in the later years of the body's existence, often from aged 60 onwards, the body's functions start deteriorating. This hampers the ability to develop consciousness. In *Back to Methuselah*, published in 1921, George Bernard Shaw argues that human beings need to live for at least three centuries in order to have time to evolve into half-decent creatures. The play was Shaw's vision of human destiny, stretching across 35,000 years, and has been considered a masterpiece of science fiction on the subject of the evolution of long-lived humans. If human bodies could last longer, then perhaps the constant recycling of souls into new bodies to allow for the soul to continue to develop might be less important.

One of the reasons extraterrestrials are visiting Earth is to work on the genetic manipulation of the human body to create a being which can last longer. During regressive hypnotherapy sessions of alien abductions, researchers have learned that human beings are being 'upgraded' as part of the next phase of development on Earth. In Dolores Cannon's *The Custodians* (1998), various regressive hypnotherapy clients stated that the intent of the genetic engineering is to create a more perfect physical body, such that the spirit, once raised in awareness, can more perfectly translate into these more perfect bodies. In other words, a more perfect spirit requires a more perfect body.

Genetic manipulation of humans has been going on for millennia since humans were first created from a blend of extraterrestrial and primate DNA. Versions of upright standing beings have been created, manipulated, amended and phased out regularly over a period of millions of years. Books such as Mary Rodwell's *The New Human* (2016) address this topic, and the creation of the human and its manipulation across millennia is summarised from multiple sources in the author's book *They Exist* (2015).

At the supreme level of Source, where souls are created, transfer of souls is considered a very important activity for soul development and is not undertaken without great care and attention to the new body proposed. Transfer of souls is only to be done in the correct dimension and frequency, which is when the soul is back in its 'home' environment in the spirit realm. It appears, however, that occasionally soul transfers can happen during the life of a human body container. A full soul transfer is different from fragments of a soul changing places during its life within a human body. Our understanding of full soul transfers comes from reporting of extraterrestrial abduction encounters where human tissue has been taken from a human body and an exact replica (a 'clone') made of that body. The soul is then extracted from the diseased or dying body and transplanted to a new clone of the body so that the soul may continue to live a longer life within the same body.

Well-known speakers, writers and therapists such as Mary Rodwell and Linda Moulton Howe have discussed soul transfer on alien crafts, as revealed during hypnotherapy sessions (although some young children do not need to recall their experiences using hypnotherapy because they have actual memory recall). In a recent interview with Mary Rodwell in November 2019 for a group calling themselves "UFOs Australia", Rodwell recounted a case of a child taken to an alien craft where the child witnessed its damaged body being worked on. The soul was extracted and temporarily housed in another (soulless) body. The child explained that the souls he observed would return to their human bodies after the work by the aliens was completed. The process entailed a 'ball of light' (the soul) being moved back into the human body, which was then reanimated and returned to Earth. The 'ball of light' is our 'essence'.

It is unclear whether the alien presence on Earth is here to help humans. There are differing opinions on this. Mary Rodwell sees the alien interaction as positive in developing a 'new human'; whereas, the well-known researcher Linda Moulton Howe argues that the true agenda of the aliens is unknown and may be negative. In an interview with an abductee, called Linda Porter, Howe reported that Porter took the view that the aliens created trauma and were using humans as a kind of laboratory for their own needs.

In her interactions with Linda Porter, Howe became aware of an alien technique for cloning humans, using 'rapid cycle cloning tubes'. Human genetic tissue is used for this purpose to allow quick growth of a new body to replace a damaged body. Porter was shown a procedure for transferring a soul from a dying man into a healthy younger cloned version of the same man, using the 'resurrection tubes'. This also happened to Porter herself, who was told by the alien that she must continue in the same genetic body container that she had been born with in order to accomplish an unknown alien agenda.

Howe reported that Porter had the impression that this soul transfer procedure was not allowed by a higher authority, but that the aliens were occasionally using it anyway and interfering with the higher purpose for their own unknown reasons. Howe has been told by her contacts that the aliens cannot enter the dimension where the soul goes on death of the body, which is why some soul transfers occur outside the dimension souls go to on death.

One explanation of this 'body-to-body' transfer of the soul from a scientific perspective has come about as a result of a recent medical advance. This advance relates to a surgical operation called a hemispherectomy, when either the left or right brain is removed. It was discovered that there is no memory loss after one of the halves of our brain is removed. This suggests that long-term memory is held in the mind ('consciousness'), not the physical brain.

Memories and the mind appear, therefore, to exist in non-physical form, in a subtle energy that permeates the physical body. Near-Death Experiences (NDEs) and Out-of-Body experiences (OBEs) provide ample evidence that the mind can exist independently from the brain, and regressive hypnotherapy can access this source. Under hypnosis, memories from consciousness take on a holographic form and can be viewed much like a three-dimensional, wrap-around movie which can be viewed from different positions, paused, and analysed. Similarly, the life review on death and NDEs can be like a holographic movie replaying one's life.

This is borne out by the work of Dr Stuart Hameroff, who was referenced earlier. He states that consciousness (the mind and, therefore, memories) is a non-localised phenomenon. It resides in the brain's microtubular structure, providing a link between the brain and the soul. Therefore, the memories can't be destroyed and move with consciousness into a new body in a parallel world (which some would call the 'spirit realm'). This is the body-to-body transfer of the soul.

Clear Proof of Reincarnation

Notwithstanding this fundamental problem of definitively showing how the soul transfers from body to body, astounding evidence of reincarnation has been compiled, even though it might be beyond rational explanation. It is perhaps some of the best evidence of a 'return to life' after death.

Reincarnation researchers such as Dr Ian Stevenson (3,000 cases) and Carol Bowman (1,000 cases) have collected impressive evidence suggesting people do reincarnate, sometimes quite quickly after their previous death. The stories often have accurate past life recall. Dr Stevenson has suggested that memories, habits, and even birthmarks can be carried over from past lives.

The evidence is so overwhelming that Dr Stevenson, a physician and scientist, who died in 2006 after a lifetime pursuing relevant cases all over the world, could never understand why his evidence suggesting the reality of reincarnation could not be accepted by others. His constant refrain was: 'How can scientists who professed to hold no dogma that reasonable evidence cannot overturn, ignore volumes of reasonable evidence that I have provided'? It is clear that his evidence *is* reasonable, and verifiable. Similarly, the regressive hypnosis work of Dr Michael Newton and the practitioners of the Newton

Institute have been factually verified in many instances. Newton's very first case of a soldier dying in the First World War was verified through the British War Office and the Imperial Museum and showed categorically that the client had been a British Sergeant and had died in 1916.

Towards the end of Dr Stevenson's life, he invited a journalist, Tom Shroder, to join him on trips to Lebanon and India to witness his investigations and interviews with children and their families where the children had clear spontaneous past life recall. Following the trips, Shroder produced a fascinating book, *Old Souls*, which was published in 1999.

The thing which became clear from Tom Shroder's work with Dr Stevenson was that the people the children remembered really *did* exist, and the memories that the children claimed really *could* be checked against actual lives, and the identification verified by credible witnesses. For the previous forty years, Dr Stevenson, who had been the Carlson Professor of Psychiatry at the University of Virginia Medical School, had been examining records in scientific journals and books, interviewing witnesses and measuring results against possible alternative explanations all over the world.

This work, which had been mainly in third world countries, was physically exacting, as Shroder reveals with great pain and horror in *Old Souls*. It is hard to imagine the conditions they worked in to obtain their information. Shroder's tales of travelling around India and Lebanon with Stevenson and his recounting of the danger of the roads, the hygiene, the accommodation and the tense situations in which they found themselves, would have sent even hardened travellers running for the nearest airport to get home. The sheer physical stamina alone required to compile thousands of cases was astonishing.

The spontaneous, waking memories of small children who recalled past lives often included names, addresses, and intimate details from lives that the children had no apparent way of knowing about. Surviving family members could be located and the child's memories checked against known and recorded facts. The facts were painstakingly verified. This was scientific; yet, scientists refused to acknowledge his work. These children were making statements as soon as they could speak, about obscure strangers and communities that were not known to the child's current parents, and at an age when fraud or hoax was realistically not possible.

Memory, even in a person's current life, is imprecise, but details revealed by many of the small children were incredibly *precise*. An example in Lebanon concerned the case of a five-year-old girl called Suzanne Ghanem. She recalled her life as Hanan Mansour, the mother of three children who died after hospital surgery. She was able to identify her past life relatives and her husband without any prompting. The five-year-old Suzanne asked her 'husband' from her previous life what had happened to the jewelry that she had given to her uncle while she was in hospital before she died. She had made specific requests about the jewelry which no one else could have known. The uncle and husband confirmed the truth of what she said. The same occurred with cases in India. When a young child saw her former husband or brother, she climbed up into their arms and clung to them spontaneously. She was able to name all the relatives and point them out, and ask why certain relatives or siblings weren't there. The reunion, like many similar, developed into lifelong friendships, despite all the hurdles involved, such as new marriage partners and new in-laws.

From all the cases, one thing emerged regularly: People who remembered past lives appeared to have died in their immediate past life through shock – accident, violence or some other trauma. This seems to be the catalyst for child remembrance, at least the children with vivid memories. A person who died peacefully in a past life rarely has a recall. In talking to Shroder, Stevenson said: "Maybe remembering is a defect. Maybe we're supposed to forget, but sometimes that system malfunctions, and we don't forget completely."

So vivid are these memories that the child thinks that they are still that 'previous personality'. They want to go back to their previous family. They don't like particular foods, they express specific wishes about what they want to do, and often go as far as to say that their current parents are not their 'real parents'. They don't say, as Shroder noted, that "the previous personality had three cows", they say "*I* had three cows". Many return (reincarnate) to a location close to where they had previously died. Stevenson examined bizarre cases in Burma where the children wanted to "return to Tokyo", hated the spicy food and the climate which was too hot, and wanted raw fish and to dress like Japanese people. These Burmese cases also assisted the debunking of the theory that the families and their children manufactured cases to support a belief in reincarnation. This is because the Japanese people were hated in Burma, where occupying troops had committed many atrocities. The last thing the Burmese parents would want to suggest was that they were harbouring the reincarnation of an Imperialist soldier.

But it seems there is never enough evidence to persuade the sceptical. It comes back to the mechanism for transfer of the personality and memories. No one knows how that happens. Stephenson's work, even with its extraordinary level of factual verification, perhaps could not go far enough to prove the existence of past lives beyond doubt. This is largely because of the question of 'what a soul is' and how it transfers from person to person. No one knows this fundamental information.

Stevenson was continually disappointed with the attitude of most scientists. He said: "For me, everything now believed by scientists is open to question, and I am always dismayed to find that many scientists accept current knowledge as fixed forever". He felt that the current generation had to literally die off before attitudes would change. Even though Stevenson had produced evidence beyond reasonable doubt, it was never enough.

Dr Stevenson's work was continued in his final years and beyond his death by Dr Jim B. Tucker who is Bonner-Lowry Associate Professor of Psychiatry and Neurobehavioral Sciences at the University of Virginia and Director of the UVA Division of Perceptual Studies. Dr Tucker published a book on his work entitled *Return to Life* in 2013. Like Dr Stevenson, he is a physicist/scientist. Also, similar to Dr Stevenson, and unlike many scientists, he is interested in the metaphysical. In his book *Return to Life*, he states that he got involved with Dr Stevenson's work because he wanted to figure out for himself whether life after death might be possible.

Dr Tucker's book explores fascinating cases of past life memory recall much like Tom Shroder's book *Old Souls* did. One case he reviews, with which he was personally involved, is that of James Leininger. This case, perhaps the most famous Western case of past life recall is reviewed and summarised shortly as it is so incredible. However, Tucker extends his discussion into metaphysics rather than limiting discussion to the exacting process of verification of 'previous personality' recall.

His discussion of metaphysical issues covered a number of areas related to the wider issue of past life recall. In one case Dr Tucker explored in Thailand, a girl's strong attachment to her previous family at the time of death appears to have affected her experiences after death and may have contributed to her memories of that life carrying over into her new incarnation. So, in addition to those lives that ended through violence, shock or other trauma, powerful attachments which are unable to be released at death may cause past life memory to carry over. As has been noted earlier in these notes, all attachments should be fully let go at death. Dr Tucker reiterates from his experience that our attitudes in this life may affect what we experience after we die and perhaps even whether we come back here for another life at all. Full release may allow us to move on from this third dimensional world; whereas, when lives and purpose have not been fulfilled, return may be a natural consequence.

But how does memory carry forward into a new body? A basic assumption of modern neuroscience is that the brain creates the mind or consciousness we experience. So how could consciousness, originally associated with a brain that is long since dead, enter or take over the body of a living person? As mentioned earlier, it has been theorised that consciousness goes through the brain but exists outside of it. It would be a separate entity from the brain, normally linked to it quite closely for the duration of a life, but separate nonetheless.

Mind might be thought to have two parts, one which survives death, the other being utilised while living. This 'consciousness' outside and separate from the physical brain contained in a body might be considered to be the 'soul'. This idea was propounded by F.W.H Myers, one of the founders of the Society for Psychical Research. Myers thought from his research that one part of each person was a soul that originated in a spiritual environment. It existed there *even while embodied in a life in the physical world*, and it continued there after the body's decay.

Referencing quantum physics, Dr Tucker states that consciousness is the primary force of existence, and the physical universe is secondary to it. He states that we think of our minds existing in this world, but it's actually the world that exists in our minds. This is now a well-established concept of quantum physics, where events do not occur until conscious beings observe them. Consequently, if the physical universe grows out of consciousness, there is no reason to think that a person's individual consciousness ends when a physical brain dies. It may continue after death and return in a future life.

In *Return to Life*, Dr Tucker references the story of James Leininger, whose case he investigated. James Leininger's story is told in immense detail in a book entitled *Soul Survivor: The Reincarnation of a World War II Fighter Pilot* by Bruce and Andrea Leininger with Ken Gross, published in 2009. Carol Bowman, a well-known therapist and author who works with children who recall past lives, introduced the book by stating that James Leininger's story is the best American case of a child's past life memory among the thousands that she had encountered. Normally, it is Asian cases which produce the best verifiable detail. But in the case of James Leininger, the child remembered names and places from his past life that can be traced to real people and actual events, facts that have been fully verified. The child was even reunited with people who knew him in his former life as a World War II pilot.

Once the facts of this case have been digested, it is hard to remain sceptical concerning the reality of reincarnation. Carol Bowman felt that this story would finally open the minds of Westerners to the reality of children's past life memories.

The story started with nightmares that the child had from the age of two. He kept screaming "Airplane crash! Plane on fire! Little man can't get out!" By the age of three he had told his parents that before he was born, he was a pilot who flew from a boat. He said his plane got shot in the engine by the Japanese, he crashed into the water and that's how he died.

Over time, his information became more specific. The child said he had been a pilot on the boat *Natoma*, had been shot down at Iwo Jima, and had a friend named Jack Larsen. The book is a fantastic story of how his mother and father uncovered the true verifiable facts behind his nightmares. After lengthy investigation, they discovered that a James Huston from the USS *Natoma*

Bay had been shot down in the Iwo Jima operation and that another pilot on the boat had been Jack Larsen. The child had a fascination with aircraft of the war period, and knew detailed mechanisms related to the planes, such as how the planes dropped their bombs and how to put on the pilot headgear.

The story got more and more bizarre as the young James revealed information. He told his parents how he 'found them'. This was at a big pink hotel in Hawaii where his mother got pregnant. He said he liked them and chose them as his parents as he knew they 'would be good to me'. He named his GI Joe toys Billy, Leon and Walter because these were the people who 'met him when he got to heaven'. It transpired that these three names were pilots who had previously been killed while on the *Natoma Bay*, and had all been in the same squadron, VC-81. In time, the parents concluded that their son was experiencing the life of a dead pilot James Huston, who had been shot down and killed on 3 March 1945. They discovered why the child broke off the propellers on all his toy planes: An eye witness confirmed that the plane he was flying had taken a direct hit on the engine propeller at the front of the plane. The witness was a fighter pilot who actually saw the face of James Huston as he crashed.

Finally, the parents contacted the people he had known in his past life. All the private and personal details checked out, even intimate details of his father's alcoholism and pictures kept in the loft, which his 'sister' (Anne Baron) confirmed. At a meeting of the old members of the *Natoma Bay* he was able to recognise individuals who had fought at that time. The nightmares were finally laid to rest when James Leininger visited

Futami-ko where his plane had crashed. The story is told over the course of a 300-page book, and it is a riveting read. By the end, one is left with the same feeling that the child's parents had felt: Here was tangible proof that there is something beyond death.

Turning to the East, possibly the most famous Asian case of alleged reincarnation took place in India in the early 1930's, and was later studied by one of the world's leading scientific investigators of such cases, Professor Hemendra Bannerjee, who was Director of the Department of Parapsychology at Rajasthan University. This was the case of Kumari Shanti Devi who was born on 12 October 1926 in Delhi, India, long before stories of reincarnation became widely publicised, and where the chances of falsification of the information was negligible.

When Kumari Shanti Devi was four years old, she began to talk about a previous life she had lived in a town called Muttra, a hundred miles from Delhi. The case has been described by many researchers, but Colin Wilson describes it as follows in his book *Afterlife*:

"Kumari Shanti Devi said she had been of the Choban caste, had lived in a yellow house, and that her husband had been a cloth merchant named Kedar Nath Chaubey. A retired school principal heard about the girl, and asked to meet her. The child told him of the address she had lived at in Muttra, and the principal wrote a letter there. To his surprise, he received a letter back from Shanti Devi's 'husband' Kedar Nath. He confirmed various details about his life with his former wife, and requested that a relative of his in Delhi should be allowed to talk to the child. When the man arrived, Shanti Devi recognised him as her 'husband's' cousin,

Kanji Mal, and soon had him convinced of her genuineness. When he reported back to Kedar Nath, Shanti Devi's 'husband' no longer hesitated. He rushed to Delhi, and the child flung herself into his arms. She was able to give convincing answers to all his questions about her previous existence as his wife, and mentioned a box containing a hundred rupees that she had buried in one of the rooms of their house.

On 24 November 1935, the nine-year-old girl was finally taken to Muttra by her parents; they were accompanied by three responsible citizens, - a newspaperman, a politician, and a lawyer – who went along to act as witnesses (and who later wrote an account of the case). As the train approached the platform in Muttra, Shanti Devi recognised the elder brother of Kedar Nath, who was waiting there. They then took a carriage, and Shanti Devi was told to direct it anywhere she wanted. As they drove along, she pointed out buildings that had not been there during her own life in Muttra. She directed them to the first house in which she and her husband had formerly lived – now rented to strangers. Asked by a local man where the 'jai-zarur' was situated – a word used in Muttra for a privy – she pointed to the outside lavatory. Then they went on to the house in which she had died. There she recognised various relatives, and showed that she was intimately acquainted with the house. Finally, she led them to the room in which she had buried the money. Digging uncovered an empty tin. Kedar Nath admitted he had removed the money. As they left the house, Shanti Devi recognised in the crowd outside her 'former' father and mother....."

Colin Wilson, Ian Stevenson and Carol Bowman and others have written of many extraordinary tales of reincarnation which are almost impossible to summarily dismiss. They strongly suggest that reincarnation is a reality.

One case investigated by Colin Wilson was of a man called Ray Bryant, who under hypnosis recalled six previous incarnations. What he insisted was that all six incarnations contributed something to where he is now in this life. It seems that the personality of the individual is an *evolving process* through the reincarnations. This feature, that reincarnation is an evolutionary process, is echoed by many spiritual teachers and mystics, such as Rudolf Steiner, Frederic Myers, Edmund Gurney, Alan Kardec, and Geraldine Cummins.

PART 3:

THE SOUL'S LIFE BETWEEN LIVES

Uncovering the Soul's Life between Lives and the Soul's Past Lives

Through the use of hypnotherapy, it is possible to uncover a soul's past - whether that be simply earlier in the current life of the soul, a past life the soul has lived, or the period between lives. For viewing, a good film depicting the process of hypnosis and what it can achieve is *Trance* (2013).

The brain consists of two halves: the left hemisphere dealing with logical thinking and the right hemisphere dealing with intuitions and psychic powers. Under hypnosis, the left brain is put to sleep, and the right is able to exercise these powers without the critical scrutiny of the left.

Dr Michael Newton, while being interviewed by Richard Martini for Martini's 2011 book *Flipside: A Tourist's Guide to How to Navigate the Afterlife*, stated:

When someone is in deep hypnosis, it's not something that can be programmed. Under hypnosis, people are very aware of who they are and have great insight into what they are telling you. Across thousands of cases there was consistency of reporting. It didn't matter whether a client had a deep religious belief system or not. Once we had them in deep hypnosis, they all told the same things.

Dr Newton's wife, who read thousands of transcripts of Dr Newton's clients, was finally convinced of the reality of what clients were revealing because complete strangers were relating stories about the spirit realm that were exactly the same.

Richard Martini asked Dr Newton why it is only *now* that this information about our soul's past and the soul's activities 'between lives' is becoming known. Dr Newton replied:

I think there are a couple of reasons. We've never been so over-populated in history, with so many of us running in so many directions. Second, I think it's the pervasive use of drugs, which has even reached our elementary schools. When someone is taking drugs to "escape from reality" it shuts down the soul. And thirdly, maybe the powers decided it's time to loosen up the amnesia block we all have when we come into this world so we're able to gain information that perhaps earlier was not really available.

Dr Newton states that people come in for a Life-Between-Life session for various reasons. For example, there may be a relative who has recently died, or there is emotional trauma from losing a child. The work is not to supplant therapy they should receive from a licensed trained professional, it's intended to provide them with answers about their inner being. He says that one of the things clients don't understand until they experience it, is that there is a dual nature to all of us:

We have our brain ego and we have our soul ego, and when they are combined it creates one personality and one lifetime.

Dr Michael Newton and the Newton Institute

Dr Newton is known for regressing patients into the afterlife, the life between lives and, in his 1994 book *Journey of Souls,* has detailed the process by which the soul develops through the process of accessing the "soul memory" of patients. It would be hard to question the results of his work, which was carried out with thousands of subjects over forty years or more, and no one has yet debunked his research claims (nor for that matter has the work of the other practitioners mentioned in this book). Dr Newton includes actual transcripts of hypnotherapy sessions where clients are reporting details relating to the spirit realm, and has trained other hypnotherapists in his techniques, so, there is enormous evidence available concerning the 'journey of souls'.

Dr Newton, who died in September 2016, set up the Newton Institute to train other hypnotherapists in the Life-Between-Lives method of hypnotherapy, and these newly trained practitioners are taking forward the work started by Dr Newton, giving us new insights to the world beyond our physical existence. *Other Lives, Other Realms,* a book written by Karen Joy, an experienced practitioner of this method, reveals interesting new observations, and is reviewed shortly.

It is also worth noting that thousands of people from very different spiritual backgrounds, ranging from atheists to religious zealots, under deep hypnosis all gave the *same or similar details* of what it is like in the spirit realm. Dr Newton says that his open-ended, non-directive questioning leaves it to the subject to describe what is happening, and the consistency of what is reported by his subjects is startling. He even said that people used the same words and graphic descriptions in colloquial language when discussing their lives as souls.

Journey of Souls gives important details relating to the life that souls have *between* lives, and the planning of new incarnations. It tells us clearly that death is not the end and, through multiple case studies, gives us information on where the soul goes after the body it is inhabiting dies. Subjects questioned during hypnotherapy even admit to feeling lonely on Earth because they miss their true "home" in the spirit realm and the group of friends they had there. They are on Earth purely to achieve learning and goals.

Journey of Souls is split into the following sections: Death and Departure; Gateway to the Spirit World; Homecoming; The Displaced Soul; Orientation; Transition; Placement; Our Guides; The Levels of Souls (beginner, intermediate and advanced); Life Selection; Choosing a Body; Preparation for Embarkation; and finally Rebirth. These stages of the soul's journey into and out of the 'spirit world' are all detailed through extensive case studies. A brief overview of the journey is set out below, based on the case studies detailed by Michael Newton.

The soul's journey on death

Immediately following death of the body, there is a euphoric sense of freedom and aura of brightness around the person. Souls float around their dead bodies trying to touch solid objects which dematerialize in front of them and, where deaths have been traumatic, there is often a desire to tell loved ones that everything is fine, though this is most often inhibited by the emotional trauma of the living. They are finally pulled away in what has come to be known as the 'tunnel effect'. Following experiencing the tunnel and arrival, there is a short process where spirits make tranquil mental adjustments before a sense of relief flows in and they realize they are back home in their beautiful world again. Advanced souls may have little adjustment to make. It should be noted that souls often leave their human hosts moments before actual death when their bodies are in great pain. There is nothing wrong with this. However, they do initially stay close by the dying body. The soul feels no remorse for committing suicide to bring a life to an end when there has been chronic physical pain or almost total incapacity. But otherwise, depending on the circumstances, suicide may be regarded as a failure to meet the life's plan by the soul's guides, the elders and soul groups on returning to the spirit realm. Nevertheless, it may be that a review of the decision to end the life is regarded favourably because spiritual advances were made before the life ended.

Our guides, soul-mates and friends meet us at the gateway reassuring us and facilitating our swift readjustment. For a very advanced soul, the welcoming party may be unnecessary or very limited because much spiritual comfort may not be required. Communication is done telepathically except very private thoughts which are shared through 'touching communication', which is "electrical sound impulses". Some souls require greater recovery on arriving back in the spirit realm if their life on Earth was particularly difficult. The recovery areas for returning souls involve some orientation back into the spirit realm. Reorientation may be intense or moderate depending on the condition of the soul. The soul is immersed in healing beams of positive energy as part of the recovery. This allows the soul to reunite with those parts of its energy left behind when it entered its last life. A preliminary debriefing of the life just completed is usual. Later on there is more in-depth counselling with guides in group settings and with the Council of Elders.

There is no separate residence for those that have conducted evil on Earth. Such a soul will have to return to Earth to endure karmic growth, often through choosing to serve as the victim of another person's evil acts in the next life. This way the soul can better understand the consequences of their conduct and witness the other side of the event. A guiding principle in the spirit realm is that wrongdoing, whether intentional or unintentional on the part of the soul, will need to be addressed in some form in a future life. However such souls do undergo separation on arrival for orientation with guides. This allows for re-structuring of self-awareness with these souls.

After arrival, the meetings with loved ones, and a short period of readjustment, the soul is then taken by its guide to a space of healing, for examination by the guide. The soul will usually appear before the Council of Elders before re-joining the soul's own soul group. The de-briefing and review work from the life just completed will be very transparent as no deception is possible because of the use of telepathy. Dr Newton states that the spirit realm (or spirit 'world' as he calls it) is a place of order, and the Council of Elders exemplifies justice. They are not the ultimate source of divine authority, but they appear to represent the last station of beings responsible for souls still incarnating. These wise beings are stated to have great compassion for human weakness and infinite patience with our faults. We go on indefinitely until we master our faults. During the time we are meeting the Council of Elders, there is an overwhelming feeling of an even higher force which Dr Newton's subjects call "the Presence". They stated that "this is as close to God as we get".

So they can plan properly for our future, the Elders want to make sure that we totally understand the consequences of our actions, particularly towards others. As many spiritually aware commentators such as David Icke and Steve Taylor have said, lack of empathy towards others is the root of the problem. If we have empathy with the consequences of our actions towards others, that is going to stop us doing anything which would adversely affect another. The lust for wealth and power and the inability to empathise are the root causes of warfare and social conflict.

Dr Newton's view is that the infinite patience of the Elders relates to the likelihood that the average soul would simply give up and not come back. Souls have the right of refusal to return to Earth it seems.

The interface between the soul and the human body

A critical question is how we felt our host body served us. Did it help or hinder development? The interface between our soul mind and the human brain is carefully analysed. The Elders know our past record with other host bodies. This includes the control, or lack of it, we exercised over the baser natures and negative emotions of bodies on Earth. Souls never offer compulsions, illusions, or attachments as excuses for their conduct.

Souls consider themselves to have finally arrived home when they re-join familiar classmates in group settings and the work of analysis of their past life and their conduct commences. It seems that everyone has a designated place in the spirit realm at their appropriate level of awareness. Often soul group members will reincarnate as relatives or close friends in the next life. We all have one or more guides who will assist and support us both in the spirit realm and during incarnations when we leave the spirit realm. These guides will never give up on us, and will watch over us, however hard our lives may be, and however many mistakes we make.

It is hard for spirits to return to Earth for further learning, but when the decision has been made, they go to the place for life selection where they can see the next life they can choose to live. This choice will be based on the desired learning experiences and will be assisted by the guides and elders. Before embarkation, the soul will revisit the Council of Elders, and then return down a 'tunnel' (as the soul did on its last departure) and into the body of the baby residing in its mother's womb. The new bodies we choose will always have risk attached to the choice, as we cannot always anticipate, for instance, what defects a body/brain may have as life develops or what the impact of the existing nervous system/emotions contained within the body will be. We will be aware of the physical appearance and general characteristics and intelligence of the body though. Some "accidents" or "damaged bodies" are anticipated and form part of the learning experience for that life.

Return to life and the people we meet along the way

People we agree to meet at certain times in a life will have a purpose attached – for example, learning, love and simply checking in to see how the soul is doing. Recognition of kindred spirits is usually straightforward. Meetings are never random or by chance either. There is one main course of life we choose in advance, but alternatives always exist and we learn from them, too. When our current life seems confusing or painful, if we stop and think, we should be able to see the direction or path our life was intended to take. Pain is always a feature of learning, however - at least on Earth.

When we review our most recent past life, we are our most severe critic. With the help of our spiritual counsellors and peers, we decide the proper mode of justice for our conduct. During our lives, guides only want the best for us and sometimes that means they must watch us endure much pain to reach certain objectives. Guides cannot assist our progress until we are ready to make the necessary changes in order to take full advantage of life's opportunities. Some people find the idea hard to believe that we voluntarily chose or agreed to the family or parents we associate with for a lifetime. However, *Journey of Souls* points out that there is usually some karmic purpose for receiving pain or pleasure from someone close to us.

Dr Newton's subjects told him that in the spirit 'world' no soul is looked down upon as having less value than any other soul. We are all in a process of transformation to something greater than our current state of enlightenment. He also states that there certainly is structure in the spirit 'world', but it exists within a sublime matrix of compassion, harmony, ethics and morality far beyond what we practice on earth. There is a value system of overwhelming kindness, tolerance, patience and absolute love.

Karen Joy: Other Lives, Other Realms

Karen Joy, a Newton Institute practitioner, wrote a book of case studies from her experiences, *Other Lives, Other Realms* (2012). It gives a new perspective on what Dr Newton himself discovered. Karen Joy notes that many people experience doubts during their regression, thinking what they are discovering could not possibly be true. However, these clients are always surprised and reassured when their subsequent research validates what they saw in the regression. They also begin to trust they will continue after their current physical lives come to an end. One client said, "With this hard evidence, something shifted inside me. I cannot deny it anymore. I surrender to the idea that I have lived before".

As a result of the guiding of many people through regressions, Karen Joy came to the conclusion that our experiences in one life can indeed influence our following lives. Many issues flow down from one life to another until the issue is resolved and cleared away. Her clients had all the usual issues that we carry through from life to life: letting go, learning to trust, realising we don't have to always be in control, releasing the fear of being hurt, or trusting to love without being hurt, and releasing unhelpful emotional energies where these energies derive from a disturbing past life or traumatic death. She found that where a person is 'off track' with his life's plan or purpose, that person is unlikely to be happy. She says that they come to the therapy saying they are lost, depressed, anxious, unsure of their direction and struggling with procrastination and lack of motivation.

According to Karen Joy, it is clear from her many regressions that we souls plan our lives on Earth before we arrive in the body we have chosen. Our soul selves meet with others to plan our lives. Then our soul incarnates to put the plan into action. At this point, it is not clear how it will work out, because on Earth we have free will and there will be many obstacles and distractions which will compete for our attention. We encounter many temptations that can throw us off track. If we are not able to grow or get forward movement any more, we will leave the physical realm and return to our spirit realm for further planning, direction and counselling.

As with Dr Michael Newton's findings, Karen Joy reports there is a process we go through after death. Healing appears to be automatic when we arrive in our life-between-lives realm. As soon as we arrive, we are taken to a centre where all heaviness and pain is released. Then we meet our Council of Elders for 'de-briefing'. The Council will provide insight into the occurrences where a person is upset by the events that occurred in the life. For instance, Karen stated in one case that the Council made it clear that the early death of the person in that life was due to the contract she made before she incarnated. There were good reasons for the death, even though the individual didn't see it that way. The Council stated that:

"There can be disagreements between the individual soul and the physical person. The contract is made by the soul. Your physical self might not agree with the contract as you play it out. You, as a human, can get very involved on the earthly plane, too involved. You can get very serious about what you are doing on Earth. You forget that life is a game. You don't really die. When you get it, you know it is all just a game. Then you can change anything in the past. The past doesn't influence you anymore. At the end of the day, the past is nothing more than multiple points of view. Nothing is concrete. You can change it."

Karen Joy states that people who undertake past life or life-between lives regressions often lose their fear of death. There are two reasons for this: Firstly, they experience dying in their past lives and, secondly, they discover where they go after death. We choose our own death, just like we choose to incarnate at a particular time, location and in a particular body.

Nevertheless, Joy is clear that preparation for death is advisable. We should do our best to ensure a peaceful death through preparation and attaining an attitude of acceptance. When death comes, she says, even unexpectedly, it only takes a split-second to release and let go.

Memories of the Afterlife: childhood

Aside from the incredible work of Karen Joy, a number of other Newton Institute practitioners contributed stories to a book entitled *Memories of the Afterlife* (edited by Dr Michael Newton and published in 2009).

One area of our lives which causes most people some level of trauma, is their childhood. Many people feel that their childhood has left them with difficulties which have a varying level of impact on their ability to lead a balanced and meaningful life while they are adults. These events of childhood, such as mental or physical bullying by parents, lack of care or love, or abandonment, need to be surmounted during adult life in order for that adult life to progress smoothly.

The Life-Between-Life (LBL) Newton Institute hypnotherapist Lynn McGonagill wrote in *Memories of the Afterlife* that "memories of childhood illustrate wonderfully how our early years groom us for our adult challenges. Many people seem to feel their childhood was difficult and even painful. When they realise we choose our parents, siblings, and earthly environment, they exclaim, "Oh no! Not me! I would never have chosen that for myself". Yet, when placed into the context of their life's work – their soul's plan for their life – each person's unique childhood is the perfect preparation for that work."

Many of the stories in *Memories of the Afterlife* revolve around overcoming painful childhoods. This relates to the need to gain courage, to release fears, to gain confidence and self-esteem, self-worth and self-value. We can sometimes look back on childhoods and ask ourselves: Why did that happen? Why was I put through that horror? There will always be a reason. It goes back to the soul's plan for that life. If we step back and think, we can work out why things happened the way they did during childhood. What lesson were we trying to learn or perfect? Perhaps we have spent many lives being undermined by more dominant personalities around us. So, we need to develop courage and strength to combat bullying and aggression, and to stand up for ourselves and learn to not be afraid. This requires us to undertake painful lessons during childhood to develop these traits. These are tests we prepare for our soul's personality, so that we can develop spiritually.

Sometimes we need to learn from tragedy. A female client of Lynn McGonagill's stated that following her LBL hypnotherapy session, she realised that life doesn't end at death. We don't need to fear death. She said "I sensed the real importance of this life was for me to realise the manner of death was insignificant, that although I had been raped and murdered, I felt nothing and was unscathed when I returned home [to the spirit world]. It was important for me to realise that this was the same for [her son] too [who was tragically murdered while driving his taxi]. Despite how horrific his whole death scene was, he did not feel it and returned to heaven unscathed, whole and clean. It did not matter." As many others have recounted, death is not a painful process.

Dr Joel Whitton's pioneering work

The work of Dr Michael Newton and the Newton Institute practitioners has been discussed at length, but an equally distinguished pioneering practitioner of the art of Between-Lives hypnotherapy was the psychotherapist Dr Joel Whitton, who wrote about his findings in his 1986 book *Life Between Life*, together with author Joe Fisher. This work preceded Dr Newton in publishing information about the life-between-life period by almost a decade. However, Dr Newton's work was far more detailed and covered thousands of cases compared to Dr Whitton's mere thirty.

Dr Whitton asked his patients under hypnosis about their memories before this incarnation - in other words, before they were born in this life. All Dr Whitton's patients were able to recall previous existences. Like Dr Newton, Dr Whitton's most interesting discovery came when he regressed subjects to the period between lives: a light-filled realm where there was no such thing as time or space as we know it.

In his book, his investigations about life between lives showed that the plane of existence we inhabit during this period is the ultimate reality - the plane of consciousness from which we embark on successive trials of incarnation and to which we return at the death of the body. On being awoken, after reviewing their life between lives under hypnosis, patients have said that now they understand that this world we inhabit in a physical body is "not the real world".

According to Dr Whitton's subjects, part of the purpose of this period "between lives" was to allow them to *plan their next life*, to literally sketch out the important events and circumstances that would happen to them in the future. As Dr Newton discovered, during this phase, the patients operated with a heightened moral and ethical sense, and no longer possessed the ability to rationalize away any of their faults and misdeeds. Consequently, the patients would recall that they would choose to be reborn with people that they had wronged in a previous life so that they would have the opportunity to make amends for their actions, what one might call pre-birth 'contracts' or 'agreements'. They planned pleasant encounters with 'soul mates', individuals with whom they had built a loving and mutually beneficial relationship over many lifetimes, and they scheduled "accidental" lessons to fulfil other lessons and purposes.

Life between Life practitioners experience no barriers when their clients are under hypnotherapy. This distinguishes this work from those people who were recalling Near Death Experiences. Kenneth Ring reported in his study of NDE experiences that those experiencing NDE's are told "it is not their time yet" and are sent back to earth for more physical living. On resuscitation, the subjects of near-death experiences often speak of having approached a "border" or "barrier" which they perceive as the frontier between life and death. Dr Whitton's subjects encounter no such restricting influence on their journeys into the next world because the transition has been completed.

Past Lives

In terms of reaching a mass audience, it was a book written by the eminent Dr Brian Weiss in 1988, *Many Lives, Many Masters* which brought the subject of a soul having lived in other bodies as part of a *learning process* into mainstream thinking.

Weiss' work on past life therapy started when he asked a patient under hypnosis ("Catherine") to go back to the time when the problem started, and was surprised to find that she had gone back to a time before this life; discovering the *origin* of the problem was the cure for it.

An interesting feature of the hypnosis sessions that Dr Weiss conducted with the patient called "Catherine" was that she intermittently accessed the guidance provided by higher spiritual beings ("masters") who gave explanations of some of the issues being uncovered as they were revealed. Amongst other things, the masters said:

"We choose when we will come into our physical state and when we will leave. We know when we have accomplished what we were sent down here to accomplish and can get nothing more out of this lifetime."

Learning appears to be a key factor in spiritual advancement, the development of the soul. Dr Weiss asked of the masters, "Why do we come back to learn? Why can't we learn as spirits?" The reply was that there are different levels of learning, and some learning must be learnt in the flesh.

"*We must feel the pain. When you are a spirit you feel no pain. It is a period of renewal. When you are in physical state, in the flesh, you can feel pain, you can hurt, and you can experience relationships which you learn from. In spiritual form you do not feel. There is only happiness, a sense of well-being. Our body is just a vehicle for us while we are here. It is our soul and spirit which last forever.*"

Another eminent past life hypnotherapist, Dr Helen Wambuch, discusses past lives in her book *Life before Life* (1978). She discussed cases of regressive hypnosis taking patients back to their past lives. But, unusually, she also discussed the concept of planning for a future life by taking that concept a stage further, by actually *progressing* people into future lives. (The immediate future life is chosen during the inter-life period, as discussed earlier). In fact, the deeper one goes into a soul's past, we discover that there is only "now time", as past, present and future are one. Chet Snow, a psychologist who worked with Dr Wambuch, continued Dr Wambuch's work after her death, and detailed his findings in a subsequent book *Mass Dreams of the Future* (1993).

This project was undertaken over a number of years and the findings are from about 2,500 people who participated in the project. The results indicated that nearly everyone agreed the population of Earth in the future was much smaller than it is today. In addition, the participants had four different views of the future. One group described a joyless and sterile future in which most people lived in space stations, wore silvery suits and ate synthetic food. Another reported living happier and more natural lives in natural settings, in harmony with one another, and in dedication to learning and spiritual development. A third group described a bleak mechanical future in which people lived in underground cities and cities enclosed in domes and bubbles. And a fourth group described themselves as survivors living in a post-disaster world which had been ravaged by some global disaster. These people lived in urban ruins, caves and isolated farms, wore plain hand sewn clothing often made of fur, and hunted to obtain food.

These four versions of the future are perhaps 'potential futures', depending on how the human race develops. Any one of the four options could be 'created', or perhaps they will all exist together or at one time or another.

Living In “The Matrix” (Hologram)

Michael Talbot wrote the ground-breaking book *The Holographic Universe* nearly three decades ago, and it is still as fresh and relevant today as it was then, perhaps more so, as we know so much more about quantum physics now. The book propounds the view that we are actually living in a hologram, and we move between changing holograms.

Dr Kenneth Ring, Professor Emeritus of psychology at the University of Connecticut, proposed that the near-death experience could be explained by the holographic model. Ring states that such experiences, as well as death itself, are really nothing more than the shifting of a person’s consciousness from one level of the hologram of reality to another.

Indeed, David Wilcock, the well-known author and speaker, asks the question: Are we living in a lucid dream? Some NDE experiencers have stated that death is like waking up from a dream. Robert Stanley has suggested in many recent interviews that the world we live in is just a ‘computer game’ in which souled and un-souled beings interact in a game created by our Controllers.

The “game” of life (the term “game” is even used by the god-like Council of Elders to refer to souls living in a human body when members of the Council of Elders were questioned during regressive hypnotherapy sessions of Newton Institute practitioners) was depicted in a modern setting in the 2006 film *Revolver*. In the film, the hero just kept *revolving* in the cycle of life until he learnt that he was just in a game. Only then could he start to *evolve*. This is exactly how the soul develops.

While living at this level of existence, we can briefly shift 'reality' but we can't change it entirely while living in the 'computer game' (The Matrix). Is the life we lead here just one big computer game? This concept of life as a computer game was depicted in the film *The Matrix* and *The Thirteenth Floor*, from Daniel Galouye's book *Simulacron-3*, where people jumped from one simulated world, a seemingly real world, to another, and then another. The films *Existenz* (1999) and *Inception* (2010) jump between different 'realities', as does *Vanilla Sky* (2001), the remake of *Abre Los Ojos (Open Your Eyes)* (1997), the subject of which is the power and importance of the mind in our reality, dreams, implanted memories and different 'realities'. All of these films make us think: "What is the 'real world'?" Does it matter whether it is a 'dream' or 'reality'? Should we care? In the end, whatever the reality, our souls go home to *their reality*, which is the alternate (more pleasant) holographic world we originally came from.

Michael Talbot quotes David Loye from his book *The Sphinx and the Rainbow* where Loye references our holographic existence:

"*The Earth is a kind of playground in which one is free to experience all the pleasures of the flesh provided one realises that one is a holographic projection of a....higher-order spatial dimension.*"

Talbot goes on in the conclusion to *The Holographic Universe* to state that:

"as long as the formlessness and breathtaking freedom of the beyond remains frightening to us, we will continue to dream a hologram for ourselves that is comfortably solid and well defined".

Souls will download into human body 'hosts', which will be either newly born babies or foetuses that are still in the mother's womb, in a procedure where they leave the spirit realm for a new life of learning on Earth. This is the 'download' back into the 'computer game', the Matrix.

Souls usually get so involved in their new lives that they quickly forget it is just another game to assist development. There is no need to get anxious or live in fear, as it is only a game. But we do, because we often forget to listen to our soul's messages, to think 'at the soul level', as we are usually influenced/driven by the ego/personality of our human hosts.

What is reality? Are we just playing at a game in order to learn, changing parts and bodies sometimes? Perhaps some people can 'tune in' to other dimensions better than others (or other levels of the computer game) and, consequently, can 'see' things that others can't. The author himself experienced 'time slips' where for just a moment he saw an earlier version of 'reality', fields where buildings are now, older buildings where new ones are now, before being transported back to the current 'reality'. This happened more than once.

Andrew Mackenzie wrote a book about 'time slips' called *Adventures in Time: Encounters With The Past* (1997) based on actually stories recounted by people of moving back in time and then returning suddenly to the present day, like walking in a field and suddenly witnessing a battlefield and dead bodies before returning to seeing grazing cows.

UFO sightings may be just that: something some people can see and not others, as they enter 'another reality'. This was Karl Jung's view.

And seeing ghosts: Some people can see them and others can't, as some people can step though veils that separate dimensions. Colin Wilson's view, from a book he wrote about poltergeist and ghosts (*Poltergeist, 1981)*, was that these incidents imply that the world around us is not as real as it looks.

Wilson's conclusion from it all was:

"if instead of this vast façade of triviality that surrounds us, we could become aware of the complex realm that lies on the other side of [this world], we might stop wasting our lives".

Linda Moulton Howe wrote in her book *High Strangeness* about frequencies when discussing the abduction of Linda Porter by aliens. Under hypnosis, Porter recalled that:

"the universe is built on sound patterns, which is why so many different worlds/dimensions can exist in the same space. Each is on a different frequency....there are countless different worlds/dimensions occupying the same space without being aware of one another, because of having their own octaves".

This makes sense, and our afterlife is probably simply another frequency. As our consciousness and vibration change, we change aspects of our existence. Death is simply another frequency.

In every day existence, most people tune out the right brain activity and concentrate solely on survival, getting by, avoiding the intrusion of any high strangeness. Survival takes all, or most of, people's time and energy and the few people who are looking beyond every day survival and raising consciousness through gnosis, acquiring spiritual knowledge, are, in the process, changing their vibration/resonance/frequency, and upgrading their consciousness.

The UFO phenomena is, as Colin Wilson points out in *Alien Dawn*, another way of raising our consciousness, of inducing change in us. People drawn into that world, whether as abductees, contactees or simply as researchers, are opening their minds to new realities, and are changing through it.

Wilson concludes in *Alien Dawn* that the human race (or some of it anyway) is about to make a transition to a state the alien visitors have already reached. Wilson does state that the aliens are not going to reveal themselves and make things easy, as positive intervention would be self-defeating. Humans must take the steps to raising consciousness themselves.

It is apparent that we can download information from The Matrix to increase or access knowledge when our minds are ready (known as 'synchronicity'). Information and messages will simply appear on cue. In the end, as Robert Monroe said after his out-of-body experiences, the mind is the key: *'As you think, so you are'*.

PART 4:

THE SOUL'S JOURNEY ON DEATH

Crossing Over and Coming Back to tell us about their experience

There are many ways that a researcher can discover that there is life after death, all of which are mentioned in this book. They range from Tibetan masters, who can surf through the dimensions of the mind and report on what death is, to shamans crossing dimensional and consciousness boundaries, past life regressive hypnosis, research into reincarnation, the reports of mediums, clairvoyants and healers, and channellers who actually witnessed spirits materialising and explaining what happens after death of the physical body.

One way most people can get an immediate 'handle' on life after death is by talking to a person who has crossed over and then returned to tell us the story. These are people who have gone through a 'near-death experience'. People who have an NDE *actually cross over and journey beyond death*. Their experience is called 'near-death' because they returned to tell us about it, *but the reality is that, clinically or medically speaking, they died*. The classification or criteria for 'death' was met by these people.

Another way is through regressive hypnosis into our life-between-lives and past lives. Yet another is the reports of ascended masters who "lucidly died", returning in another body to tell us about it, as detailed in books such as *The Tibetan Book of the Dead.*

Past lives, life-between-lives and reincarnation have been discussed previously, and the process of *actual* death, including death where the person 'returns' (the near-death experience) will now be discussed. The evidence given throughout this book should leave even doubters with the assurance of the existence of an afterlife.

There is an Afterlife: Dr Eben Alexander's *Proof of Heaven*

[Perhaps the greatest Near Death Experience of all.......]

Dr Eben Alexander is a well-known brain surgeon and scientist who once believed only in the 'here and now'. To him, life after death was an absurdity, as he 'knew' that all so-called 'otherworldly experiences' when people had 'near-death experiences' was brain-based, and 'consciousness' was not possible without a working brain.

What happened to Dr Alexander, as he described in his 2012 book *Proof of Heaven*, caused him to completely revise his science-based views, and become more spiritual in his approach to life. It is reasonable to suggest that the events that occurred to him were 'divinely sent' as there can hardly have been a person living who was better placed to provide 'proof of heaven'. This was a doctor who understood the workings of the brain better than almost any other living person, and who had conducted surgical procedures on the brains of hundreds of patients.

Consequently, when his entire neocortex (the outer surface of the brain, the part that makes us human) shut down and completely ceased to function when he contracted a rare brain illness, the scientific-side of Dr Alexander would have come to only one conclusion: He was dead.

In the past, he would have distinguished his condition from those of other near-death experiencers by saying that in those other cases the neocortex only *temporarily* shut down, but remained essentially undamaged as oxygenated blood flow was restored in a timely manner. In his case, the brain shut down for a period of time that rendered him clinically dead, such that he encountered the reality of a world of 'consciousness' that existed completely free of brain activity. Now he understood that their near-death experiences were just as real. They also were 'dead' during their experience.

What this proved to Dr Alexander was that the death of the body and brain is not the end of consciousness, and that 'human experience' continues beyond the grave.

Moreover, in a statement that is remarkable for a previously die-hard scientist and materialist, he stated that our lives continue after death "under the gaze of a God who loves and cares about each one of us and about where the universe itself and all the beings within it are ultimately going". This echoes the evidence presented in Barham & Greene's *The Silver Cord*.

Dr Alexander's experiences as a 'dead person' can only be properly understood by reading his remarkable book. He met persons and entities that were of a higher spiritual level who gave him messages that were comforting to all of us still living and who will, of course, one day undergo the experience, the event, of death. The main messages were that 'we are loved and cherished, dearly, forever'; 'we have nothing to fear'; and 'there is nothing we can do wrong'.

More importantly, what became clear is that *the mind is the key to life after death.* Dr Alexander could extract himself from an unpleasant experience, or project himself to a beautiful place, or instantaneously receive answers to questions he had. Everything was telepathic. Thought is the key to the post-death experience.

Dr Alexander discovered something very important during his journey out of body: that unconditional love was at the centre of our universe, although evil was necessary, because without it free will was impossible.

We need to learn, to experience and to grow spiritually. There are many dimensions to experience as we grow, as Dr Alexander was able to discover as part of his 'tour' of the spiritual realms.

There is no terror that we should feel about death. We are never separated from Source ('God') during our stay on Earth, and that is a major cause of anxiety. At the back of our thoughts we always wonder what will happen when we die.

Dr Alexander's ability to go deep into the next world after his death was helped by not having any memory of who he was on Earth. He had no memory of his loved ones here. There was nothing he was 'leaving behind'. No attachments to extract himself from. Nothing to mourn. This allowed him access to the cosmic being he is beyond his earthly body. (We are all cosmic beings.)

To go deep into the spiritual realms beyond life on Earth, we must release our attachments to whatever level we are on before we can go higher or deeper. The reality for Dr Alexander, though, was that it was more painful to *return* to Earth after the existence he encountered while 'dead'.

The brain contains what he calls a "reducing valve" to filter out knowledge of the higher (non-physical) worlds, which is necessary in order to survive on Earth in the 'here and now'. We need to experience and learn at the earthly level in order to grow towards the Divine (a growth that is closely watched by the beings in the worlds above, who help us during our earthly existence), and knowledge of the world above would simply slow down progress. We wouldn't want to be here.

Dr Alexander suggests we use our time here to get closer to our true spiritual self, rather than build up some ultimately worthless fame, wealth or power. How do we do this? According to Dr Alexander, by manifesting love and compassion. In order to successfully return to the spiritual realm, we must become *like* that realm.

For a scientist who could not believe the concept of 'life after death', his conclusion after his experience is incredible:

"For all the successes of Western civilisation, the world has paid a dear price in terms of the most crucial component of existence – our human spirit. The shadow side of high technology – modern warfare and thoughtless homicide and suicide, urban blight, ecological mayhem, cataclysmic climate change, polarization of economic resources – is bad enough. Much worse, our focus on exponential progress in science and technology has left many of us relatively bereft in the realm of meaning and joy, and of knowing how our lives fit into the grand scheme of existence for all eternity".

Proof of Heaven helps to explain where we are going. It should come as a relief to all who doubt that the spiritual realms exist.

Another extraordinary NDE: Anita Moorjani's spontaneous healing

Anita Moorjani should be dead, according to an experienced oncologist, Dr Peter Ko, who examined her medical notes after she returned from her NDE. Yet not only was she alive, but within days she had completely recovered from her terminal lymphoma cancer, which had devastated her body. This 'spontaneous healing' (or 'spontaneous remission' as Dr Ko called it) can only be described as a miracle. The doctors who witnessed it could not believe that the tests after the NDE showed no sign of cancer in a patient previously overtaken by cancerous tumours. Anita Moorjani recounted her NDE on near death websites and got sufficient notice, as would be expected from such an unusual occurrence, that Hay House approached her. The result was an excellent book published in 2012 entitled *Dying To Be Me*. It became a bestseller and shot Mrs Moorjani to worldwide fame.

Her book is less about the NDE itself (unlike Dr Eben Alexander) and more about the effect on her and what it all meant. Naturally, the book focuses primarily on the causes of the illness and how it left her body subsequently. She appears to have experienced something which would normally happen only following death: the immersing of her body in the all-loving, all-healing, Source. This cured her. She merged with the Divine.

Dr Ko wrote a report which stated that the chemotherapy which was given to Moorjani at the time of death was not the cause of her cure. He speculated that 'something non-physical either switched off the mutated genes from expressing, or signalled them to a programmed cell death'. Her organs had shut down at the time she was admitted to hospital so, as far as the doctors were concerned, she could not recover. Her family had even been informed that the fight was over. Yet, something caused them to start functioning again. The doctors wanted to know who flicked the switch to turn the body around from dying to healing. The reality is that the Source of Life cured her so she could come back and tell us.

Anita Moorjani's etheric body, also called energy body, was healed – not her physical body. As is made clear in the book, she was shown how illness starts, which is not in the physical body, but in our energy body. If we cure that, the physical body naturally follows. We cure ourselves at a spiritual level. What became clear to her is that drugs can rid the illness from the physical body, but unless the energy body is cleared too, the illness will inevitably return. Physicists such as Richard Gerber, who wrote *Vibrational Medicine*, and William Tiller, concur with this view.

Moorjani was very clear about what caused her illness. It is a universal problem with living, and can be summed up in one word: *fear*. We go through life worrying about failure, whether we are liked, getting ill, death - the list is never ending. When everything we do is designed to win approval of others, rather than focusing on what is right for us, we get sick eventually. Our energy is eaten away. Often, as in the case of Anita Moorjani, a person is wrapped up in cultural expectations, whether that be religious, social, family standing, behavioural requirements as a man or woman, or what the 'hive mind' thinks. Eventually breakdown can occur. Our parents have been so programmed by their parents and their surroundings that they have forgotten that their children are people who need to follow the appropriate path for their talents. That is overlooked in the need to conform and what is expected of them. As Moorjani said in her book, what she now understands is that she is at her most powerful when she allows herself to be who life intended her to be. She now lives her life from joy instead of from fear. When we are happy we are healthy. And, the external world mirrors what we feel about ourselves: People can see happiness and sadness. We should not live our lives to constantly please others at our own expense. We must follow our path.

As with almost all other experiencers of NDEs, Moorjani changed after the NDE. The fear of life (and death) had gone. She understood better the folly of people neglecting all the things that mattered, such as relationships, love, and our true path, just for money. Like Michael Singer has previously emphasised about our energy, Anita Moorjani started to let negative thoughts pass through her with acceptance and without judgment rather than suppressing her feelings. This allows the emotions to pass harmlessly.

The NDE of Anita Moorjani is similar to many others we can read about: She felt calm, peaceful, healed, all pain, sadness and sorrow was gone. She was completely unencumbered from her past. Above all, she was encompassed by a pure, unconditional love. All love was unconditional. Love was everywhere.

Jodie Long, the editor of a book of exceptional NDE stories entitled *God's Fingerprints: Impressions of Near-Death Experiences*, emphasises that love is the overwhelming impression which emanates from the NDEs. She says:

"The biggest way that knowledge of unconditional love affects people is the way that people treat themselves and others around them. When they realise that love is all there is and that is what we are judged on when we go to the other side, our priorities on earth change. We treat people with love, compassion, tolerance, patience – all the qualities that embody unconditional love."

Short Notes on the Near-Death Experience

The knowledge, or discovery, made by the 'dead' person arising out of the NDE is that everyone who goes through this experience *knows absolutely without question that there is life after death*. There is no doubt about it in their mind. They don't need what men of religion would call "faith". That would imply *doubt*, and for experiencers, there is *no* doubt. They *know*. NDE's are based on solid knowledge and facts, and as the *near-death.com* website states, the only rational conclusion is that there is life after death. Faith and scepticism becomes the irrational viewpoint.

After an NDE, it is unanimously reported by experiencers that they have lost their fear of death. Their experience is usually so profound that they actually look forward to returning to the beautiful realm that they encountered.

In David Wilcock's 2011 book *The Source Field Investigations*, he discusses out-of-body experiences. It seems from research undertaken concerning the out-of-body experience that, on near-death or death of the body, the body loses weight. If the body recovers, the weight is immediately regained. Is this the soul leaving and returning?

In 1907, as published in the *American Medicine* journal, Dr Duncan MacDougall found that his patients suddenly lost a little over one ounce of weight directly after physical death. In these studies, the patients were kept on beds within a metallic basin that would catch any bodily fluids. The air they exhaled from their lungs on death did not weigh anywhere near one ounce – nonetheless the weight loss remained consistent in every case. In 1975, Dr Hereward Carrington and associates found that the average person would lose two and a quarter ounces of weight while they were having an out-of-body experience. When they returned to the body, the missing mass immediately returned.

David Wilcock states that it appears that there is an "energetic" component of our bodies that may be withdrawing from each and every cell and projecting to other locations – either at death, when remote viewing or when having an out-of-body experience.

Wilcock notes that a surprisingly high number of people who have out-of-body or near-death experiences see a silver cord that attaches their astral body to their physical body. In the majority of cases the cord appears to be attached to the exact location of the pineal gland, and emerges either from the front or the back of the head. Wilcock suggests that it may very well be that we all have an *energetic duplicate* of our physical body that is constantly travelling outside ourselves, and reporting back what it sees to the pineal gland – through the silver cord. Floating piezoluminescent crystals in the pineal gland may then release these images in a three-dimensional matrix of light. The retinal tissue in the pineal gland might be capturing these photons and sending them to the brain, where they are unscrambled into visual images if they remain stable enough.

Ancient mystery schools and religions were (and still are) obsessed with pineal gland symbolism, and have always believed that awakening this gland was the ultimate key to spiritual advancement, and the method by which the physical world we live in while occupying a human body, and the spiritual world, are connected. Buddhists, Hindus, Taoists and the Ancient Egyptians, amongst others, consider that the pineal gland is the key to spiritual awakening, intuition and the receipt of spiritual messages. It may be a key component in the coming shift of mankind.

Rene Descartes, the 17th century philosopher who wrote *The Treatise of Man*, stated: "*My view is that this gland is the principle seat of the soul, and the place in which all thoughts are formed*".

The silver cord is the means by which the soul, through the pineal gland, links with the spirit (non-physical) world. The Bible itself mentions the silver cord in Ecclesiastes 12:6 – "Remember him – before the silver cord is severed, or the golden bowl is broken."

The silver cord has been discussed earlier in this book and seems to be inexorably connected with life and death. The disconnection of the silver cord from the physical body represents the arrival of death and the return to the spirit realm to which the physical body was connected through the silver cord. The silver cord is our spirit body's "lifeline" to our physical body in the same way that our umbilical cord is our "lifeline" to our mother's body during the birth process. Babies are born into the world with an umbilical cord connecting them to the life-giving source of the mother which is disconnected by doctors after birth so the baby can live independently.

A surprising number of people experience a continuing consciousness when they are clinically dead – again suggesting that some part of our thinking mind is strictly energetic, and does not need a physical body at all. In order for a person to be considered clinically dead, the heart has to stop beating, the lungs stop breathing and there is no measurable brain activity due to lack of oxygen. By conventional medical account, our minds should no longer function – or even exist. However, a variety of people have reported having vivid near-death experiences during this time. Many people continue to be able to observe their environment and think normal thoughts while they are clinically dead, showing no brain waves whatsoever. Dr Sam Parnia, Dr Pim Van Lommel, Dr Raymond Moody and Dr Kenneth Ring and others have concluded from their studies that being clinically dead does not interrupt the continuity of our thinking minds.

As with the Tibetan teachings, it appears from the reports of NDE's that life and death are *in the mind itself.*

In the Greek, Egyptian and other ancient eras, it is reported that people in secret societies were given 'controlled' NDE's, chemically induced psychedelic experiences on par with the accidental nature of NDE's. These experiences were kept secret and to this day are referred to as "mysteries", such as the Greek Eleusinian Mysteries. These are explorations of a reality that exists beyond the threshold of what we see and experience in our everyday reality. The 1990 film *Flatliners* is a good introduction to the concept of chemically induced NDE's, which assist growth of the spirit.

Michael Talbot, in *The Holographic Universe*, states that people who have undergone NDE's often describe going through a "passageway to the land of the dead". He argues that the similarities between near-death experience and the *Egyptian Book of the Dead*, an ancient Egyptian funerary text from nearly 4,000 years ago, which is sometimes translated as "The Book of Emerging into the Light", are more than coincidence. That book documented the journey of the soul through the underworld and into the afterworld, or afterlife. Talbot's conclusion from his research is that people who have undergone NDE's are not suffering hallucinations or delusional fantasies, but are actually *making visits to an entirely different level of reality*.

Raymond Moody, author of the best-selling work *Life after Life*, reported that people who have experienced NDE's state that the experience dramatically changed their lives. They usually became a "new being". Often, material pursuits were traded in for more spiritual goals, and they ceased to have any fear of death. NDE's have been well researched now, and the majority of experiencers have reported a positive experience. Kenneth Ring identified five stages that are commonly reported: peace, body separation, entering darkness, seeing the light, and entering the light. Additionally, some go through a black tunnel (gate) to enter into brilliant white light, experience intense feelings of unconditional love and acceptance, meet beings of light and loved ones, and receive a life review. Some receive knowledge about life and the nature of the universe.

This 'core experience' is repeated consistently by people undergoing an NDE. Kenneth Ring said he would 'remove his white lab coat and describe his own beliefs – for what they may be worth'. He stated that "I do believe – but not just on the basis of my own or others' data regarding near-death experiences – that we continue to have a conscious existence after our physical death and the core experience does represent its beginning, a glimpse of things to come". This was brave on the part of a scientist to make such statements which at that time several decades ago would have attracted ridicule.

One aspect of the NDE is the many reports of a 'life review' that occurs with 'beings of light'. These reviews demonstrate inescapability of karma and the far-reaching and powerful effects of all our actions, words and thoughts. The message is always the same, that the most important qualities in life are love and knowledge, compassion and wisdom.

There is no reason why we have to undergo an NDE to lose our fear of death. Just reading about the experiences of those who have had an NDE should be enough.

Pre-Death Experiences

In her book *On Life After Death*, Elizabeth Kubler-Ross discusses her work with dying children. What she discovered over a long period of time as a psychiatrist was that thousands of people all around the world share the same "hallucinations" prior to death. These "hallucinations" relate to the awareness of some relatives or friends who preceded them in death. She considered the best way to verify that these hallucinations were not simply a projection of wishful thinking was to sit with dying children after family accidents. She said this often happened after special weekends such as the Labor Day weekend in the USA when families get together and end up in multiple-death car crashes and survivors brought dying to the hospital. The children have not been informed that any of their relatives have been killed. Near to death, the children are overtaken by a peaceful serenity, and it was at this time that Elizabeth Kubler-Ross would ask if they are willing to share what they are experiencing at that time just before death.

Kubler-Ross stated that the children share words such as the following: "Mommy and Peter are already waiting for me". Kubler-Ross stated that she was aware that the Mommy had been killed but not that Peter had also been killed. Then later she received a call to say that Peter had just died. She stated that in all the years that she had collected this kind of data, she never met a child who in the imminence of their own death mentioned a person in their family who had not preceded them in death, even if only by a few minutes. This extraordinary fact helps to confirm the existence of a life following bodily death. These children that Kubler-Ross talked to were already aware of the presence of their deceased family members who will wait for their own transition. Then, they are reunited in a different form of life that many need persuading of its existence.

Many of these dying patients, old and young, experience the presence of beings who surround them, guide them, calm them and help them. These presences have been called guardian angels, guides or, in the case of young children, playmates. Kubler-Ross is sure that all souls, from the moment we end our physical existence and then transition, are in the presence of these guardian angels or guides who wait for us and help us in the transition from physical life to the life we will have after death. She also states that we will always be met by those who preceded us in death who we loved.

The guides are very important. Kubler-Ross was talking to an old lady who was in her last days, who said to Kubler-Ross "Here he is again". When asked for further explanation, the old lady said when she was a kid 'he' always played around her. But until now the old lady had forgotten that 'he' existed. A few days later the old lady died, full of joy, knowing that someone who loved her dearly was waiting for her. Many small children have spirit playmates, who they talk to and are fully aware of their presence. But on going to school, parents tell the children to forget their childish 'playmates'. As a consequence, these 'friends' are usually forgotten until the children are dying, when often they return to guide the dying person over to the other side.

Nurses have often talked of patients seeing the light *before* actual death, and in a large number of reported cases, the dying believed they saw a deceased relative on the point of death. Dr Karlis Osis, who was the Research Director at the Parapsychology Foundation in New York was fascinated by this and had the idea of circulating a questionnaire to doctors and nurses, asking them what they had observed about dying patients. Six hundred and forty questionnaires were returned, covering more than thirty-five thousand cases. The findings were published by Osis in 1961 in a book called *Deathbed Observations by Physicians and Nurses.*

A primary observation was that fear is not dominant in most dying patients and, a surprisingly large number of patients were, in fact, elated at the time of death - even to the point of exaltation and seeing visions. The visions were often of 'heaven', or a 'promised land'. Many patients who were revived after 'dying' expressed sentiments like "I want to go back". But also, many patients talked about these visions when fully conscious and not under sedation or medication and before sliding into a death coma.

The overall conclusion was that dying people generally felt no fear of dying, and they often believed they were being met by dead relatives. This book was published before Elizabeth Kubler-Ross came on the scene, but her findings are entirely in line with the findings of Osis.

PART 5:

PARANORMAL PHENOMENA

Clairvoyants

William James, who was an influential American psychologist and pragmatist at the end of the 19th century, was a sceptic concerning the paranormal until in 1885 he met a remarkable young medium called Leonore Piper. Piper would go into trances and was taken over by her 'control', a Frenchman named 'Phinuit'. Through this dead person, Piper was able to convey extraordinarily accurate information which it seemed impossible that she could have known. Eventually, after many years of tests, James became convinced of life beyond death after information was revealed that could not have been learned through telepathy. This was a remarkable transformation to spiritualism and the belief of life after death from the founder of a philosophical school of thought known as 'pragmatism'. For him, the afterlife became fact. It was a similar 'turnaround' to Dr Eben Alexander's in *Proof of Heaven*.

The lengthy story of Mrs Piper was revealed in Frederick Myers' classic 1903 book, *Human Personality and Its Survival of Bodily Death*, released two years after his death, which became the most important work ever written on the paranormal. It revealed that spirits of formerly living persons could continue to communicate through special individuals after their death. Thus, it would be reasonable to conclude that life continues in some capacity after death. Mrs Piper was, in effect, a 'telephone line' by which the dead could continue to converse and impart vital information.

Prior to his death, Myers had often remarked that one of the few ways for 'communicators' to prove beyond all doubt that they were speaking for spirits of the dead would be to give separate bits of a message to several mediums, so that they only made sense when fitted together. This would rule out matters such as telepathy and cryptomnesia.

After his death, Myers achieved this with the celebrated series of communications known as the *Cross Communications*, which effectively proved that persons in the spirit realm could communicate with the living. Myers was able to demonstrate that the 'spirit' had accurately communicated something which could not have been known to the medium or clairvoyant or anyone else present. The communications were detailed in two books by Geraldine Cummins: *The Road to Immortality* and *Beyond Human Personality*.

Rudolf Steiner, an accomplished medium who could sense 'unknown modes of being' around him and communicate with the souls of certain dead persons, asserted that the dead needed to communicate with the living to nourish their beings.

Unfortunately, the clairvoyant ability that existed in former times enabling a direct link between the living and dead so that the living could follow the progress of the dead relatives in the afterlife had been lost over time.

This ability could, Steiner believed, be recovered if the world became more spiritual again. Steiner's own ability to follow the progress of certain dead persons in the spirit world gave him the information which made him a valuable mystical source. Steiner firmly believed, and stated in his writings, that the world of the mind *is* the spirit world.

The importance of dreams

In a lecture given by Rudolf Steiner entitled "*The Dead Are With Us*" he maintained that the best time to ask the dead a question is before going to sleep.

He stated:

"We encounter the Dead at the moment of going to sleep, and again at the moment of waking....These moments of waking and going to sleep are of the utmost significance for intercourse with the so-called Dead – and with other spiritual beings of the higher worlds. The moment of going to sleep is especially favourable for us to turn to the Dead. Suppose we want to ask the Dead something. We can carry it in our soul, holding it until the moment of going to sleep, for that is the time to bring our questions to the Dead....On the other hand, the moment of waking is the most favourable time for the Dead to communicate with us." Steiner considered that the Dead were always present, it was just a matter of finding the method for communicating.

Emanuel Swedenborg, whose book *Heaven and Hell* was discussed previously, also used the borderland between sleeping and waking for his most important communications with the Dead. Thomas Jay Hudson stated that the subjective mind works best on the point of sleep because it is then free of its usual domination by the objective mind. As Colin Wilson put it in *Afterlife*, the right cerebral hemisphere is freed from its usual domination by the left-brain self.

When we are in pain or sorrow, it will help to tune in to our guides and become aware of their presence. The guides that are always with us can be asked questions before we go to sleep, and be asked to answer us in our dreams. Those who have been tuned in to their sleep states, to their dreams, become aware that many of our questions are answered in this state. It is our all-knowing inner self, our soul support team, that helps us. The often unknown people who appear in our dreams are part of a 'film' we are making in our sleep. This is to assist us to assimilate what is happening during our waking time. It is a different reality, but no less real or meaningful than our time in a waking state.

To assist in the preparation for death, the Tibetans suggest we should practice the art of lucid dreaming. This is the art of dreaming while being aware that we are dreaming. Professor Thurman, an expert on Tibetan Buddhism, says that if we can train ourselves to become self-aware in dreams, it will be easier to remain lucid in the dreams that are the 'bardo states' (the Tibetan stages of death).

Bizarre Communications through Automatic Writing

In his book *Afterlife*, Colin Wilson discusses at length many methods by which the Dead communicate with the Living and, after reading the 300-page book, it is hard not to be convinced of the existence of an afterlife. Wilson himself was left in no doubt of its reality after carrying out immense research and examining the facts available in detail.

One unusual method of communicating is a technique called 'automatic writing' which was favoured in the 19th century. One of the most famous cases was that of the author Sir Arthur Conan Doyle, author of the Sherlock Holmes stories who, in his later years, was ridiculed (by no lesser people than Winston Churchill, Lloyd George and King George V) for his conversion to Spiritualism after witnessing the ability to communicate with the dead through automatic writing. One day, Doyle was sitting at the bedside of a dying friend watching her produce automatic handwriting. He was startled to recognize the writing of his brother-in-law Malcolm Leckie, who had died at the battle of Mons. Doyle began to asked questions, and 'Leckie' replied. Doyle asked him a particularly difficult question about a private conversation they had had before the war. The reply specified precisely what he and Leckie had discussed. Yet, Doyle had mentioned it to no one else – not even his wife. From then on, he had no doubt about the reality of life after death.

One of the saddest stories of anti-spiritualist prejudice recounted by Wilson concerned an architect called Frederick Bligh Bond. In 1907, the ruins of Glastonbury Abbey were bought by the nation, and Bligh Bond was appointed to take charge of the excavations. As Bligh Bond was a devotee of spiritualism and the ability to communicate with the Dead, he decided that his task would be greatly simplified if he could contact some of the long-dead monks of the abbey and ask them where to dig.

A friend of his, John Allen Bartlett, was able to produce automatic writing, so Bond rested his hand on his friend's pen and asked questions, with Bartlett's hand writing out the answers. When Bond asked where a missing chapel had been situated, Bartlett's hand drew a plan of the abbey with the chapel on it. The 'communicator' called himself 'Gulielmus Monachus' – William the Monk. And when Bond's team dug to the position indicated, they found the chapel. His employers, the Church of England, were delighted. They continued to be delighted as Bond made find after find, including another chapel. Bond took care to tell no one that most of his information came from William the Monk and various other 'communicators' who called themselves 'the Watchers'.

Finally, in 1917, he decided his success had justified itself, and told the whole story in a book called *Gate of Remembrance*. The Church was not amused and Bond lost his job, even being refused admittance thereafter to the precincts of the abbey.

However, the evidence speaks for itself and, years later, the Church of England stated that the doctrines of Spiritualism *were* consistent with Christianity, as Christians did believe in a life after death.

The case of the materialisation of a dead person: Elizabeth Kubler-Ross and Mrs Schwartz.

The proof for life after death has been provided in abundance earlier in this book. Materialisation from the spirit realms was mentioned in Barham & Greene's *The Silver Cord*, but it is worth also mentioning the story told by the famous psychiatrist and physician Elizabeth Kubler-Ross, recounted in her book *On Life After Death* concerning the materialisation of Mrs Schwartz, a patient of hers who had died.

Mrs Schwartz, who had undergone a Near-Death Experience which brought her to the attention of Kubler-Ross, had been dead about ten months when she re-appeared *in the flesh* before Dr Kubler-Ross. Dr Kubler-Ross had decided to cease her lectures on Death and Dying at the University of Chicago and was standing at the elevator when the dead woman appeared in front of her. She said "Dr Ross, I had to come back. Do you mind if I walk you to your office? It will only take two minutes."

Dr Ross considered she must be hallucinating as how could she be walking to her office with a dead person?

She decided she had to touch her to know if she was real. Mrs Schwartz opened her office door and said she had to come back to tell Dr Ross that she should not stop the work on death and dying, not yet anyway, because it was too important. Dr Ross sat down at her desk and touched her pen, chair, desk to confirm they were real. She hoped Mrs Schwartz would just disappear, but she didn't. She just stood there. So Kubler-Ross asked if she could sign a note for their mutual friend Reverend Gaines.

Dr Ross gave her a piece of paper and a pencil so she could have proof that Mrs Schwartz's appearance was real. Incredibly, with a loving smile, the dead person took the paper and wrote a note. Then she asked "Are you satisfied now?"

She then got up and made Dr Ross promise not to stop her work. Dr Ross did that and kept the note safe thereafter. At the time she wrote the book *On Life After Death*, she still had the note. Dr Ross subsequently became one of the most famous practitioners in the field.

PART 6:

SHORT NOTES ON THE PROCESS OF ACTUAL DEATH

An initial note about death

As Patricia Cori states in *The Cosmos of Soul*, true spirituality builds upon a basic understanding and acceptance of the death process. It is the surrendering – the dissolution of matter as it transmutes into light – that is the key to the meaning of life on all dimensional levels. Many ancient spiritually advanced cultures on Earth, such as the Tibetan Priesthood, the Maya, and the Native Americans, prepared for the death process from the first moments of their arrival in physical form. Rather than fearing death, they explored and trained for it, so that the passing would be familiar, when time called them back through the tunnel – the metaphysical reflection of the tunnel of life known as the birth canal.

The mirror, identical process, the returning to the light, is much less traumatic than the coming into matter: The death canal. One doorway leads in, and another leads out, only the "in" door moves from light into the density of the physical passageway of the vaginal tunnel, while the "out" door, the portal of the liberated soul (freed from the limitations of physical existence), exists only as a multidimensional doorway from which the soul expands from the dense material back to light, releasing from the crown chakra.

Cori suggests that our greatest terror as physical beings is fear of death, the fear of nonexistence. The fear is that the ending of life will bring some ghostly existence as mere light waves floating out there somewhere in the Cosmos. That deep, unresolved fear is a subconscious memory of passing over the grey zone, where we move and shift through the various birth and death experiences of our reincarnational cycles. The grey zone lies between dimensions, between states of being. Every time we pass through the tunnel of death and birth, we are confronted with the void and must move quickly over it. We know the danger, for it is as close to nonexistence as we can come in an otherwise vibrantly moving and expanding universe.

On death, Cori states that the body must be left in silence while still carrying the song of the soul. The music must have ceased in the tissues and fluids of the body. Transplants of still-living organs are not advisable because if there is still enough life force to be transplanted, then the body is still carrying the soul frequency and must not be disturbed.

In his outstanding book *Healing Lost Souls (2003)*, William Baldwin reiterates that the transfer of body parts is inadvisable due to soul fragmentation.

The spirit-manifesting body never intended to be artificially attached and superimposed into the vibrational blueprint of another being, whose desire (imposed or otherwise) to cling to physical life denies the soul process originally set forth before incarnating (an excellent film depicting what can happen after a transplant of body parts is the film *21 Grams* (2003).

The desire for transplants is indicative of human misconception and fear of the death process, which is still viewed as The End.

In reality, death is part of a normal process of soul development, an evolutionary experience, rather than the end of life.

Dr Elizabeth Kubler-Ross' clinical findings about death

Dr Elizabeth Kubler-Ross reports, from her research, that as soon as our soul leaves the body, we will immediately realise that we can perceive everything happening at the place of dying, be it in a hospital room, at the site of an accident, or wherever we left our bodies. We do not register these events with our earthly consciousness, but rather with a new awareness, even though clinically our bodies are dead. We understand and can see everything that those around us do, say or think. Humans are not able to see the soul which is out of physical body while conversely, the stepped-out soul can still register earthly vibrations, and (as an example) can understand everything that happens at the site of an accident.

In the period immediately prior to death, or in the period after a person has just been declared dead, that person can still hear everything we say. Thus, at these moments it is not too late to say "sorry," or "I love you", or whatever else we want to say. In this way, we can unburden ourselves of guilt so that we may thereafter live more fully.

At this stage the 'deceased' person will realise he is whole again. People who were blind can see again.

People who couldn't hear or speak can do these things again. People who couldn't walk can dance again. We have been told these things by those undergoing a near-death experience. Dr Ross realised that none of this information would appease a sceptic. She therefore did a scientific project with blind people. The condition was that the experiment would only involve those blind people who had not had any light perception for at least the last ten years. The out-of-body experience of this category of blind people who came back could state in detail what colours and jewelry someone was wearing who was present. They could tell the pattern of a sweater or tie. These are indisputable facts. They could see again! Raymond Moody, in his 1977 book *Life After Life*, confirmed what Dr Ross was saying that a recurrent feature of the OBE's was the perception of a 'new body', shaped like the physical body that had been left behind but *free of all the defects*.

As well, it was revealed that nobody can die alone. There are people waiting for us who died before us, who loved and treasured us a lot. Every human is guided by a spirit entity from his birth until death. In general, the people waiting for us on the other side are the ones who loved us the most. Where those who love us most are still alive, our guardian angel will receive us. After the initial meeting with a guide or guardian angel, the dead person will be turned over to others who will continue the assistance. Moody's observation on the events that occur on death were almost identical to Kubler-Ross' observations.

After death, and before we exchange our physical earth form for our non-physical form, we pass through a phase where we see visions that are from our physical world. Robert Bruce states that the deceased appear to be held in the astral real-time zone by residual vital life energy. During this time the deceased will typically frequent areas, homes and people they were familiar with during their lives. When this vitality is used up, spirits fade away and move on to the next stage of their existence. Kubler-Ross says that at this phase, or perhaps at the end of this phase, it could be that we float through a tunnel, pass through a gate, or cross a bridge. We are then embraced by light. This light is whiter than white. It is extremely bright and the more we approach this light, the more we are embraced by unconditional love that is indescribable. In this light, we look back on our entire life from the first day until the last.

With the viewing of our lives, we reach a third stage. On this level we are no longer in the possession of consciousness from the first stage, or awareness from the second stage. We are now in possession of knowledge: We know in minute detail every thought we had at any time during our life on earth. We remember every deed and know every word we spoke. We know every consequence resulting from our thoughts, words and deeds. We will understand why events happened as they did, which was to allow us to grow spiritually, to allow our souls to develop. We will realise it was wrong to have become bitter or angry.

It is worth reiterating that although our biggest fear is to die alone, at the moment of transition, we are never alone. Indeed we are never alone in our earthly physical lives, although we don't normally realise it. But at the time of transition, our guides, our guardian angels, people who have passed on who loved us will be there to help us. This has been scientifically verified beyond a shadow of doubt.

The Crossing from Life to Death

The crossing on death back into the spirit realm is something that has always been a mystery, something we have probably done before but have no recollection of. We die, but then how do we really get back 'home', to the safety of our friends and guides in the spirit realm? Is the crossing difficult? In Dr Michael Newton's *Life Between Lives*, multiple clients have actually described the crossing during their regression hypnosis.

The speed at which a soul will leave behind the body he or she used for this life will depend on the strength of attachment to people, possessions, location and so on, as well as the level of advancement of the soul. Once the full realisation of the death of the body has occurred, and the soul has let go of its surroundings, the soul will then commence the journey home, moving higher and higher and further and further away from Earth.

Dr Newton often asks his clients a simple question: "Does the space around you get lighter or darker?" The older souls tend to immediately move into bright light, bypassing 'the tunnel' with the speed and eagerness they have to 'get home'. The soul will instinctively know the speed at which it should move as it adjusts to the changes following physical death. A soul may enter a portal or tunnel, as it did on the way in, experiencing a short period of darkness first, depending on the circumstances of death and familiarity with the journey home and spirit realm it is heading for. Dr Newton says there is no precise formula or reasoning behind this process, but all souls arrive safely. The tunnel may be a period in which the soul may still turn around and return to life, as near-death experiencers often recount.

Whether the client recounts drifting through darkness, greyness, or clouds, the key is to keep moving, as all scenarios are normal in the transitional journey home. Dr Newton tells his clients "You have been this way before. Just keep moving and accept the fact that a loving power is taking you to a safe place".

Soon the soul floats into a space where they can see into the distance, and will report seeing lights. These lights may be bright and close by or some way off into the distance. These lights *represent intelligent beings*. A larger single globe of light close to the soul typically represents a spirit guide, while points of light in the distance are typically companions from the soul's own spirit group. If a soul is advanced, it will be able to direct itself towards the lights without assistance from guides. The mind can direct the soul's progress forwards or in any other direction towards the lights. The colour of the lights may vary depending on the advancement of the person meeting the newly arrived soul. Once linked up with a guide, the soul is home.

Neale Donald Walsch – *Home With God*

The renowned writer Neale Donald Walsh, who has sold millions of books in his series *Conversations With God*, wrote a final book in the series entitled *Home With God* (2006) which is a perfect introduction to the subject of death. The revelations contained there about death induce a feeling of calm and comfort.

Walsch maintains that his information comes directly from God, or Source, and that this is who he obtained his extraordinary level of detail on death and the after-life from. However, the information almost certainly came from a higher level of his consciousness, the 'knowing part' of his consciousness that is not limited by physicality, which some call supraconsciousness or superconsciousness. It is a remarkable talent to be able to access this level of consciousness so clearly, in so much immense detail, that he is to be able to write books about what is revealed from this level of higher consciousness. Even so, we can all receive clear messages if we listen to our deep instincts. The information contained in the book is so perfect and easy to follow that it is difficult to question the findings he has described. Much of his information is, in any event, backed up by other sources, many of which have been quoted in these notes.

A key reassuring piece of guidance is: "All souls find peace after death. Not all souls find peace before it."

But Walsch's book does contain some unique pieces of information. There are a number of features that are not found in the vast numbers of books on the afterlife. A key point he emphasises is that we normally have an intuition about the time of death as we *choose* the method and time of our death. Although we may not consciously realise it, we decide the moment of our death. There is a choice. There is nothing to fear, even if it is sudden. We know that our death has a purpose and meaning and, bizarre though it may seem, is intended to help another person – as Walsch puts it, "serves the agenda of another person". All deaths leave a message for those who remain, if we seek out the message, and listen and learn from it.

No one, however appalling the circumstances of death, ever died in vain. The death of a young child is, of course, hard on those left behind, but Walsch maintains from his sources that all souls die (the body that hosts them, that is) "in the service of the agenda of another". The soul is aware of this "agenda" at the superconscious level, beyond the conscious and subconscious levels. This is where the larger agenda of the soul is held, and where spiritual development is directed from and derives from.

Walsch says that while we are in the spiritual realm, we set ourselves learning purposes and goals we wish to achieve while in a physical body, and when this purpose or purposes have been achieved, we will die. If we try and escape those aims while living by committing suicide, perhaps because we found the goals were too hard for us, all that will happen is that we will create the same life over again in another physical body until we have learnt the lesson, and overcome whatever issue we were facing, much like is portrayed in the 1993 film *Groundhog Day*. Once back in the spiritual realm, we will give ourselves another physical life in which to deal with what we did not deal with in our most recent life.

Incidentally, euthanasia is completely different from suicide. People who commit suicide in the middle of an otherwise active and reasonably healthy life are basically 'escaping'; whereas, people who end their lives a short time away from a life that was going to end anyway are making an entirely different, valid, choice that it is unnecessary to suffer the final pain and indignity at the end of their life. Each soul has an answer that is right for it, and there is no 'incorrect' answer.

Home with God answers very clearly the most important question that we normally have: What happens following our death?

Death has three stages.

Stage one is the same for everyone. At the moment of our death, we will instantly experience that our life is over. We may have a short period of disorientation as we come to realise that we are not 'with body' anymore and are separate from it. Soon we come to realise that while we have 'died', we have not ended our life. It is in this moment that we realise and experience fully that 'our body' is not 'us'. A body is something we can *have*, but it is not something we *are*.

Immediately, we will then move into stage two, and this is where experiences will vary from person to person. The experience a person has will be the experience of whatever we believe will happen after death, whatever we expect to find there. If our belief system thinks we deserve heaven, or hell, we will experience that. Stage two is driven by the *state of our mind.* In life, we are actually creating our 'stage two' death experience. If a person believes there is no afterlife, this stage two will be like falling asleep. The good news is that *everybody* wakes up, whatever belief system applied in that life they just left behind. For such a person, the soul will awaken through the ministrations of loved ones and angels. Death is a doorway, and the energy we take through that doorway determines what's on the other side. We draw from the experiences at stage two whatever remembrances there are to draw from them, and then we will move on to stage three.

Stage Three starts with the feeling of flying at incredible speed through a 'passage' towards a pinpoint of Light. The Light is warm and glowing and safe and inviting. We are heading into the "Core of Our Being". The soul hovers before the Light, basking in the glow of the Essence. All fear or apprehension or uneasiness drop away during the race through the passage, and the Essence radiates pure love. All 'bad' and 'good' that the soul had thought of itself, all shame or pride, is slowly absorbed by the Light. The soul is being immersed in love and healing. The merging with the Light dissolves the identity the soul had from this life. We are now truly 'ourselves' again. We are not body, nor mind, nor spirit. We are all three, merged. This is what the entire death process is about.

First, at stage one, we release our body; at stage two, we release our mind; and at stage three, we release our soul. In death, all our 'identities' are shed ending the separation *of* 'us' *from* us. We are *one.*

This 'state' can also be achieved during our lives. We can simply look into our own eyes in a mirror. Do not turn away if this deep looking becomes uncomfortable. Soon we will experience incredible love and compassion for ourselves. Then close the eyes and stay with the feeling, the feeling of merging with Essence. The eyes are the windows of the soul.

On death, we remain merged with the Essence for as long as we wish, during which time we will review all the moments of our life. We can do this for as long as we like. We will not wish to be merged forever, though. The Total Immersion renews, rejuvenates and re-creates us as the identity we remember ('the core of our being'), reminding us of our agenda, and then we decide how to re-create ourselves anew and take on a new life to continue developing.

Our time in the spiritual realm is a time of great Knowing, but there will come a time when Knowing will not be enough. The soul will seek to *experience* what it Knows of itself and what needs resolving. This, the soul understands, can only occur in the physical world. We will wish to resolve 'core issues' we have, such as of not being worthy or good enough, or thoughts of insufficiency, or fear of abandonment and other issues. The soul always has a choice: a choice to live or a choice to die. Everything is our own choice. But as Walsch puts it, we should be aware that:

"Sometimes the soul chooses things at a subconscious or superconscious level that it would never choose at a conscious level. This is in order to fulfil its Larger Agenda".

Finally, on death, we will again be with all those who have held a place in our hearts and have gone before.

There is no need to worry about those we left behind, for we will see and love them again, through eternity. There is no separation where there is love. Our loved ones will guide us into the spiritual realm as we release our attachment to the physical world.

A Spiritual Path: the journey of Tibetan masters through death and rebirth

The essence of the message given by the Tibetan masters is that death is simply a process of the mind. If the mind is at peace, the process of transitioning into the afterlife is straightforward. If the mind is fighting the reality that the body has died, then the transition is harder.

A 14th century mystic, Meister Eckhart, said he had seen Hell and interpreted the key message of *The Tibetan Book of the* Dead as follows:

"The only thing that burns in Hell is the part of you that won't let go of life, your memories, your attachments. In Hell they burn them all away. But they're not punishing you, they're freeing your soul. So if you're frightened of dying, and you're holding on, you'll see devils tearing your life away. But if you've made your peace, then the devils are really angels, freeing you from the earth."

This 'battle of the mind' on death was portrayed very effectively in the 1990 film *Jacob's Ladder*. In the film, the hero had died in Vietnam, but was unable to come to terms with his death and it was only when he had gone through a necessary period of viewing and analysing of his past life that he was able to move on and 'go up the ladder'. Similarly, in the 1989 film *What Dreams May Come,* the hero had to learn to accept death and let go of attachment to his body, his family, his possessions, his career.

The Tibetan masters have worked for millennia on the formula for living and importance of the state of the mind at death. This has been transcribed in books such as *The Tibetan Book of the Dead* and Sogyal Rinpoche's *The Tibetan Book of Living and Dying* (which incorporates *The Tibetan Book of the Dead*).

The Tibetan Book of the Dead was originally transcribed by Padma Sambhava in the eighth century from testimony of adepts, and then hidden in a cave on a Tibetan mountain before being discovered in the fourteenth century by Karma Lingpa. The adepts could 'die' and remain awake ('lucid dying'). The Tibetan expert Alexandra David-Neel states that as their psychic energy remains coherent after death, they are reborn with their past memories intact, through mothers whom they have selected. She states that the experience was not a near-death experience, but an actual death and then a conscious rebirth experience. The rebirth of these masters and teachers, such as the Dalai Lamas, is revered.

The testimony of these teachers, which has filled many learned books and journals over the years, is briefly summarised in the pages that follow.

Wisdom and Ignorance

Sogyal Rinpoche, the late Tibetan spiritual teacher said:

'To follow the path of wisdom has never been more urgent or more difficult. Our society is dedicated almost entirely to the celebration of ego, with all its sad fantasies about success and power, and it celebrates those very forces of greed and ignorance that are destroying the world. It has never been more difficult to hear the unflattering voice of the truth, and never more difficult, once having heard it, to follow it: because there is nothing in the world around us that supports our choice, and the entire society in which we live seems to negate every idea of sacredness or eternal meaning'.

Thus, any focus on spirituality or good conduct is ridiculed in today's society. The six negative traits of humans, referred to shortly, are in the ascendancy.

In Buddhist terms, the very first teaching of the Master called 'Buddha' was that humans were caught in an endless cycle called 'samsara', and the root of suffering in samsara was (and is) *ignorance*. We must stop fooling ourselves. We must stop throwing away the chance that life gives us to learn. As the masters say, what will we have learned, if at the moment of death we do not know who we are?

The *Tibetan Book of the Dead,* a text written millennia ago, but still relevant today, put it as follows:

With mind far off, not thinking of death's coming,
Performing these meaningless activities,
Returning empty-handed now would be complete confusion;
The need is recognition, the spiritual teachings,
So why not practice the path of wisdom at this very moment?
From the mouths of the saints come these words:
If you do not keep your master's teachings in your heart
Will you not become your own deceiver?

Help is at hand

At death, and in the present, all the enlightened beings are present to help us, all we need to do to receive direct help is to ask.

Jesus Christ said:

"Ask, and it shall be given to you; seek and you shall find; knock and it shall be opened unto you. Everyone that asks receives; and he that seeks finds."

Yet asking is what we find hardest. The acknowledging that we have a long way to go, that we are not perfect. Sometimes it is because we are arrogant, sometimes because we are unwilling to seek help, or we are lazy to do so. It could be that we are so busy with the trivialities of everyday life and are distracted, and the simplicity of asking just does not occur to us. The turning point in healing or learning is when the individual admits their illness or ignorance and asks for help.

Helping the Dying

We often forget that the dying are losing their whole world - their house, their job, their relationships, their body and their mind – everything that makes up their 'life'. This has the effect of making most people sad, angry and fearful. Elizabeth Kubler-Ross has suggested that the process of dying falls into five mental stages: denial, anger, bargaining, depression, and finally acceptance. This also applies to the loved ones of the dying.

But the moment we accept dying, it is the opportunity to change ourselves in a positive way and come closer to our own deepest truth: who we really are, and why we are here.

One piece of extremely important advice that spiritual helpers give is never to leave unfinished business where it is possible to resolve or clarify matters prior to death. They say it is never too late to heal the pain of the past. Forgiveness and resolution of past issues is vital for a peaceful death.

Usually unfinished business is the result of blocked communication, most often being an unwillingness or inability to see the other person's point of view.

It is never too late to let negative feelings go. But more importantly, failure to do so will make it harder for a person to die peacefully, and this is important when put in the context of what the masters reveal happens after death. A dying person should not have anxieties about those who they loved and who may continue living for perhaps a very long time after they are gone. Finally, above all, a dying person should be allowed to die in silence and serenity, unaffected by invasive medical procedures or unwanted meddling.

The Moment of Death

A Tibetan Master, Jamyang Khyentse, who could journey through the dimensions of the mind, was often asked for guidance for the moment of death, as he had travelled to that state of being many times. His advice was always very simple as to what is needed as we come to die, although difficult to achieve:

"Be free of attachment and aversion. Keep your mind pure."

The Tibetans masters say that there are two things that count at the moment of death: What we have done in our lives, and what state of mind we are in at that moment of death.

Our state of mind at death is all important. *The last thought and emotion that we have before we die has an extremely powerful determining effect on our immediate future.* So the state of mind at the moment of death is extremely important.

Letting Go Of Attachment

The ideal way for a person to die is having given away everything, internally and externally, so that there is as little as possible yearning, grasping, and attachment for the mind at that essential moment to latch on to. So before we die we should try to free ourselves of attachment to all our possessions, friends and loved ones. We cannot take anything with us, so we should make plans to give away all our belongings beforehand as gifts or perhaps as offerings to charity.

If we are making bequests, such as might be made in a will, these wishes for the transfer of ownership of possessions or other desires for post-death arrangements, should be expressed as lucidly as possible. Making everything clear, down to the final details, will reassure us as we are dying, and help us to truly let go.

The atmosphere around us at death should be as peaceful as possible. This is a paramount requirement. The Tibetan masters therefore advise that grieving friends and relatives should not be present at a dying person's bedside, in case they provoke a disturbing emotion at the moment of death.

We are to release attachment, not have any reason to wish to remain attached and fight departure. Sometimes this may be extremely difficult for families to understand; they may feel they are no longer loved by the dying person. However, they should bear in mind that the mere presence of loved ones may provoke strong feelings of attachment in the dying person, which make it harder than ever for him or her to let go. If possible, it is best if friends and relatives do not show excessive grief at the moment of death, because the consciousness of the dying person is at that moment exceptionally vulnerable.

As the Tibetan master, Jamyang Khyentse advised:

At the moment of death, abandon all thoughts of attachment and aversion.

Leaving the Body

The *Tibetan Book of the Dead* is a helpful source in dealing with the process of leaving the body.

The masters, who have travelled through the dimensions of the mind many times, advise that *the experiences at death are, without exception, the projections of our own mind*. Acknowledging this is calming.

The teachings tell us that it is precisely because we no longer have a body in the spirit realm that there is no ultimate reason to fear any experience, however terrifying, that may happen to us after death. How can any harm, after all, ever come to a "no body"? The problem it seems is that even in the spirit realm most people go on grasping at a false sense of self, with its ghostly grasping at physical solidity. The continuation of that illusion, which is at the root of all suffering in life, exposes them in death to more suffering, especially in the immediate period after death.

What is essential is to realise now, in this life, when we still have a body, that its apparent solidity is a mere illusion. The realisation of the body's illusory nature is important in helping us to let go. The Tibetans say that the world of the living, which we are in now, is *also* a dream. Our experiences here are illusionary, temporary.

Inspired by and armed with this knowledge, when we are faced at death with the *fact* that our body is an illusion, we will be able to recognise its illusory nature without fear, to calmly free ourselves from all attachment to it, and to leave it behind willingly.

The Clear Light of the Mind

Sogyal Rinpoche explained that in death all the components of our body and mind are stripped away and disintegrate. As the body dies, the senses dissolve, and this is followed by the death of the ordinary aspect of our mind, with all its negative emotions of anger, desire and ignorance. Finally, nothing remains to obscure our true nature, as everything that in life has clouded the enlightened mind has fallen away. Only consciousness remains. And what is revealed is the primordial ground of our absolute nature, which is like a pure and cloudless sky.

This is called the Ground Luminosity, or "Clear Light", where consciousness itself dissolves into the all-encompassing space of truth. Padma Sambhava describes it as a "self-originated Clear Light". The light emanates from within us as we become freed from the "darkness of unknowing and become endowed with the ability to cognise".

After the initial luminosity, a second phase occurs with a brilliant dazzling light. The person will realise that he is dead. He will see his dead body and try and re-enter it, but he cannot. Sorrowful and afraid, he will realise that he cannot take anything accumulated over his lifetime: his friends, his family, his wealth, even his own body. All he has now is a 'mental body'. But he is free. He can go anywhere unimpeded. By merely thinking of a place, he can be there instantly. The deceased will now go on a journey based on the ideas in his own mind. In the words of *The Tibetan Book of the* Dead: "What you see is only a reflection of the contents of your mind sent back to you by the mirror of the void". Nothing restricts us except our own mind.

The whole landscape and environment is moulded by our own minds. If our habitual conduct in life was positive, our perception and experience in the spirit realm will be mixed with bliss and happiness; if our lives were harmful and hurtful to others, our experiences in the spirit realm will be ones of pain, grief and fear. This is not some judgment from on high, but simply the workings of our own deluded minds.

There is a waiting period before rebirth. We have to wait in the between-life world until we can make a karmic connection with our future parents.

Without a physical body to ground us, thoughts in the spirit realm actually become reality. The overwhelming power of thought is the key issue in the transit lounge before re-entering the physical world in a new body. The advice of the *Tibetan Book of the Dead* is that during the soul's time out of body, the now-dead person should study, enhance and better understand any spiritual practice that person may have had during his or her life: for instance, to give up attachment to people and possessions, not to give in to desire or anger, to cultivate kindness rather than hostility, and never to contemplate negative actions.

Further, the *Tibetan Book of the Dead* tells us that the terrifying figures we meet in the spirit realm are nothing more than our own deluded projections and by nature empty. These figures themselves only have a mental body of habitual tendencies and are, therefore, empty too. So, it says, "emptiness cannot harm emptiness".

These visions are likely to appear terrifying to those who have little awareness of their true significance. Those who have spent innumerable lifetimes believing in the reality of the outer world, and who are unaccustomed to the vibrancy and brilliance of the inner world of fundamental consciousness, will flee in horror and panic at the awesome power of the unfettered mind once it is free of the limitations of a body.

The *Book of the Dead* states:

"remember that you have an astral body and cannot really be harmed by [horrors encountered]. These demons are actually devoid of any substantial existence, for they merely arise from the creative energy of your primordial mind. Think of them as your spiritual friends and protectors come to guide you through the dangers of the transitional phase and all your fears will dissipate."

The Transitional Phase of Rebirth

There have been many commentaries published on the *Tibetan Book of the Dead*, which has been a Buddhist text for centuries. The 1999 commentary by Stephen Hodge and Martin Boord was an extremely readable commentary with the message that we can learn from the reality of death and dying to help us make more of life and living.

Hodge & Boord's analysis of the rebirth phase from the texts discusses the negative traits an individual possesses, as the individual will be directed back into that lifestyle, relating to the dominant negative trait, on his or her rebirth. They state that if the dead person fails to reform his or her actions and intentions, then the accumulated energy of repeated negative patterns of behaviour will resurface and project them into the situations and lifestyles that are most suited to such patterns.

The commentary continues by stating that it is important for us to recognise the negative emotion that predominates our personality during our lifetime, for then we can take steps to avoid falling into situations that merely serve to strengthen such negativity. If we truly feel unable to help ourselves, we can usefully turn to prayer, and ask for help from the divine compassion that shines out from enlightenment.

Our ego-minds often play tricks on us because of our propensity for particular lifestyles. Though we may rationally be aware that a particular mode of behaviour is unwholesome and will lead to unhappiness, our egos convince us that such lifestyles are attractive and pleasant. In fact, they are likely to be nothing of the sort. Similarly, the ego will want to avoid future situations that threaten its security, and so will tell you that another course of action is unpleasant and is to be avoided.

Accept what life offers us without indulging in value judgments. We must ultimately learn through rebirth to overcome the particular lifestyle propensity we have, and resolve in our new life to practice what is wholesome and will benefit others.

A Summary of the Tibetan Masters findings

Death is like life: We can never truly return to the way we were before we met with any profound crisis or conflict. We must move on, but it is up to us whether we do so in a wholesome and liberating manner or just create more of the same.

There is no judgment on death as many religions promote. Everything is a projection of the ego-mind. The dead are aware of their own failings and stand in judgment over themselves. However, they are then in danger of tormenting themselves needlessly for their past deeds, when all that it required is to renounce such negativity and attempt to cultivate the positive virtues to avoid evil acts in the future.

The key is to understand that, whether in the spirit realm or now, in this life, the process is unfolding and every moment counts. All thoughts, actions and emotions matter.

The Tibetan teachings make it clear that what happens in our mind now in life is *exactly* what will occur in the spirit realm at death, since essentially there is no difference; life and death are one in "unbroken wholeness" and "flowing movement".

Above all, everything is a projection of our own mind.

The need for cremation on death

Richard Matheson, in *What Dreams May Come*, his classic book about survival after death, discusses the attitudes of people toward those who have died. His findings mirror those of the Tibetans, the Egyptians and other races whose rituals on death go back into ancient times.

Matheson notes that since the consciousness of the deceased is so vulnerable to impressions, the emotions of those left behind can have a powerful effect on that consciousness. Intense sorrow creates a vibration which actually causes pain to the departed, holding them back from progression. Funeral ceremonies are meant to be a medium of peaceful release, not a ritual of grief.

It is said that the remains of the dead should always be cremated three days following death. This frees the departed from a tie which has a tendency to keep the soul of the departed near its former physical body. In cases of extreme attachment, where there is difficulty breaking the cord even after death, the fire severs it immediately.

People can't forget their bodies easily, after a lifetime wearing the 'tunic'. They want to continue to see the thing they once believed to be themselves. Sometimes that attachment makes it difficult to leave the earth plane. This is why cremation is important. It severs entirely any lingering attachment.

End Note: Nothing Lasts Forever

The cyclical nature of the universe is closely linked with the impermanence of all things and situations. The Buddha made this a central part of his teaching. All conditions are highly unstable and in constant flux, or as the Buddha put it, impermanence is a characteristic of every condition, every situation we will ever encounter.

When we are young, we don't think about death. We feel life is limitless. Evelyn Waugh in *Brideshead Revisited* called it the 'languor of youth' – those heady days when you are young and everything is ahead of you, when everything seems possible. We can waste as much time as we want, because there is so much ahead. But time is not limitless. We must use it well.

In his book *The Sheltering Sky*, Paul Bowles wrote that because we do not know when we will die, we get to think of life as an inexhaustible well and, yet, everything happens only a certain number of times. 'How many more times will you remember a certain afternoon of your childhood that is so deeply a part of your being that you can't even conceive of your life without it? Perhaps four or five more times? Perhaps not even that. How many more times will you watch the full moon rise? Perhaps twenty. And yet it all seems limitless'.

Eckhart Tolle recounts in *The Power of Now* what a Buddhist monk once told him:

"All I have learned in twenty years that I have been a monk I can sum up in one sentence: All that arises passes away. This I know".

APPENDICES

APPENDIX 1

THE TEMPLATE

A short template has been developed from the findings of the spiritual teachings previously referenced which may be a reference or reminder of what will help the development of a soul during its time in a physical body on Earth. This list of attributes is hard to achieve and a major reason why souls keep returning to earth to complete their learning.

In order for the soul to complete its 'tour' of the physical world, often found to be an unpleasant and testing experience, and not need to incarnate again, the soul must meet, at minimum, the following criteria:

- The soul must have the unconditional ability to "let go" of earthly possessions, connections and emotions on death.
- The soul must overcome six negative emotions: pride (hubris), jealousy, desire, ignorance (the celebration of ego and image so loved by today's society), greed, and anger.
- The soul must have no further purpose in returning to physicality.
- The soul must have developed a pure, clean heart at time of death.

Each of the negative emotions is encountered every day. These are understood and eradicated through the encounters we have during our physical existence.

Whatever way we have lived our lives, however much contrary to the spiritual path, this can be changed at any time. That is why we are here. We can change. As spiritual masters such as Paramhansa Yogananda have said, 'what we have done, we can undo'.

In *Autobiography of a Yogi*, Yogananda states:

"*None other than the person himself was the instigator of the causes of whatever effects are now prevalent in his life. He can overcome any limitation, because he created it by his own actions in the first place, and because he possesses spiritual resources that are not subject to planetary pressure.*"

APPENDIX 2

THE EXISTENCE OF A NON-HUMAN SPIRIT DIMENSION: THE ORIGINS OF OUR KNOWLEDGE OF THIS WORLD

In 2005, Graham Hancock produced one of his greatest works, *Supernatural*, which reveals evidence of the existence of a non-human spirit world. This immense work doesn't tell us where we go on death, who we will meet or what we may experience after death (though this information is revealed in the course of this book), but sets the scene as to how humans started to realise that our current physical existence is not all that there is. Historically, this goes back 40,000 years.

The spirit world or dimension addressed by Graham Hancock through his research is a world beyond our physical world that we live in now, which we will probably never encounter either in this life or after death. Our physical world is, in fact, just a part of a reality spectrum that includes unseen energies and dimensions that permeate our physical reality. The dimensions beyond this reality we exist in are numerous, involving many different experiences depending on the state of our mind, but regardless of what we actually personally encounter (if anything – and we may not be aware of any encounter that occurs) beyond this world, it is clear that there is a world beyond what we can see.

The spirit world depicted in *Supernatural* is a world we may encounter in altered states of the mind while living, but (as mentioned above) is unlikely to be a world we will go to, or encounter, on death. Encounters while living are likely to be with non-physical, or mainly non-physical, beings operating at a different energy frequency. It is important to understand the spirit world addressed in *Supernatural* as it crosses with our physical world, whether we perceive it or not.

The origins of our knowledge of the existence of a spirit world

Homo Sapiens has been around for nearly 200,000 years; yet, it was only about 40,000 years ago that humans became innovative and artistic, symbolic and cultured, religious and self-aware. This point of change occurred when humans started making cave paintings. The earliest known is at the Pech Merle caves in South-West France.

Human behaviour changed so dramatically at about the 40,000 year mark that it is almost like the arrival of another species. The interesting feature was that the stepping-up of human intellectual ability was not accompanied by any anatomical change. In particular, the human brain size did not change, remaining constant for the whole period of existence of homo sapiens. In fact, it has remained constant from the time of the ancestors of homo sapiens around half a million years ago.

What caused the momentous change of behaviour that gave birth to modern human culture? It seems that human advancement occurred from interaction with supernatural agents who inspired change.

It is a fact that every society that we have known about since the appearance of modern humans has maintained a steadfast belief in the existence of supernatural realms and beings, notwithstanding the lack of irrefutable evidence. Where did this belief, which is common ground in all religions, come from?

The conclusion seems to be that hallucinations could have given rise to early religious notions about supernatural realms and beings, and the survival of the 'soul' at the time of death of the physical body. Such ideas appear to have originally come from the visionary realms where the shamans of all cultures in all periods made their 'spirit journeys'. In these out-of-body journeys, shamans were able to meet hybrid man-beasts, light-beings, experience transformations, and have encounters with the deceased. It could be said that the birth of religion is documented inside the deep caves of Upper Palaeolithic Europe. The painter-shamans were hallucinating and painting their visions.

It was the shaman who first discovered the way to leave his body here on earth, send his spirit to the otherworld to contact and negotiate with the beings there, and then return to his body and resume normal life again. This is where the notion of soul-journeys to the otherworld first originated.

Scientists can't accept any 'otherworld' inhabited by supernatural beings. Yet, teachings that derive originally from the shamans are that these supernatural beings exist in another dimension, and we must interact with these non-physical beings, which, though generally invisible and intangible, have the power both to harm us and help us. Most people are not aware of this 'other' dimension, as once they are born into the physical world, their spirits become so attached to it that they are only able to leave it again when they die.

Hallucinogens, used by shamans since the time human behaviour changed 40,000 years ago, are a method for inducing altered states of consciousness by temporarily 're-tuning' the brain to pick up frequencies, dimensions and entities that are completely real in their own way but are normally inaccessible to us. Scientists who rule out the existence of spirits and the supernatural base their opinion on their *preconceptions* on the nature of reality rather than on direct personal knowledge (as might be obtained from the use of hallucinogenic plants which allow shamans and others to enter different realms).

Shamans and others who have entered deep trance states through the use of hallucinogens or other methods, are of the opinion that only a thin veil separates the world of everyday reality from supernatural otherworlds where powerful spirits dwell. Indeed shamans contend that the spirit world and its inhabitants are real, that supernatural powers and non-physical beings do exist, and that human consciousness may, under certain special circumstances, be liberated from the body and enabled to interact with and perhaps even learn from these 'spirits'.

It is highly possible that humans made their great leap forwards 40,000 years ago through the interaction of shamans with the spirit world and because the shamans were literally helped, taught, prompted and inspired by supernatural agents and passed that information on to the human population. These teachings then became enshrined in early religion. The cave art of the early shamanic painters documented their encounters with supernatural beings, such as the therianthrope (part human, part animal).

Aldous Huxley, in the 1950's, concluded through the use of hallucinogens, that 'the function of the brain and nervous system and sense organs is in the main *eliminative* and not productive – i.e. that these organs operate primarily as a 'reducing valve' that protects us from being overwhelmed by a mass of useless knowledge, allowing us to stay sane and alive. Certain persons, however, *'seem to be born with a kind-of by-pass that circumvents the reducing valve. In others, temporary by-passes may be acquired either spontaneously, or as the result of deliberate 'spiritual exercises', or through hypnosis, or by means of drugs. Through these permanent or temporary by-passes there flows....something more than, and above all something different from, the carefully selected utilitarian material which our narrowed, individual minds regard as a complete, or at least sufficient, picture of reality'.*

In 1983, the Swiss scientist Albert Hoffman, who first synthesised LSD, noted: *'The entry of another reality under the influence of LSD, may be explained by the fact that the brain, the seat of the receiver, becomes biologically altered. The receiver is then tuned into another wavelength than that corresponding to normal, everyday reality. Since the endless variety and diversity of the universe corresponds to infinitely many wavelengths, depending on the adjustment of the receiver, many different realities...can become conscious.'*

Hoffman goes on to state that the true importance of LSD and related hallucinogens lies in their capacity to shift the wavelength setting of the receiving 'self', and thereby evoke alterations in reality consciousness. This ability to allow different, new pictures of reality to arise, this truly cosmogenic power, makes the cultish worship of hallucinogenic plants as sacred drugs understandable.

The key point appears to be that anything which gives the receiver the ability to change his wavelength and to access 'higher spiritual agencies' needs to be given attention.

William James uses the expression 'higher spiritual agencies' as something that can be encountered when changing our consciousness or awareness allows us to go through certain doors in the mind. He says '*The hubbub of the waking life might close a door which in the dreamy Subliminal might remain ajar or open....if there be higher powers able to impress us, they may get access to us through the subliminal door*'.

In 2001, a leading American psychiatrist, Rick Strassman, of the University of New Mexico, published the results of the first federally approved and funded human hallucinogen research in the USA in over two decades. The results forced Strassman, like Aldous Huxley, Albert Hoffman and William James to consider the possibility that hallucinogens might change the receiver wavelength of the brain, allowing it to make contact with 'unseen worlds and their residents' that are opaque to us in normal states of consciousness but, nonetheless, completely real. Strassman says '*It takes only a second or two – the few heartbeats that the 'spirit molecule' [DMT] requires to make its way to the brain – to change the channel, to open our mind to these other planes of existence*'.

Today's focus is on 'aliens' and 'alien abduction', where under hypnosis people recall episodes of abduction by 'extraterrestrial beings' who took them up in spaceships in the sky or underground or underwater and did painful humiliating and unpleasant things to them there. However, this is simply another, very modern, way that certain people have accessed a different reality under trance conditions, as Hancock explains in detail in *Supernatural*.

The encounters with fairies and, recently, 'aliens' of all descriptions (animal, reptilian, humanoid, insectoid etc.) and the depiction in cave paintings 40,000 years ago of supernatural 'states' through artists entering into trance conditions are not encounters in the physical world we inhabit in our human bodies on a daily basis. These encounters are conducted in an altered state of consciousness where the encounters are with non-physical beings (even if there may be occasionally traces of 'physical encounters' on the human body after the encounter is over). No aliens are actually 'visiting from outer space' so they cannot be described as 'extraterrestrial'.

Hancock lays out irrefutable evidence that since the beginning of modern human behaviour 40,000 years ago, humans who encounter spirits in trance states have frequently and graphically reported 'procedures' which Westerners would term 'medical' or 'surgical'. Whether it be shamans, cave artists who depict piercing and spearing of 'wounded men', or fairie encounters or alien abduction, the same story is told time and time again. What is the common link between spirits in one part of the world and at one period of history, and aliens in another part of the world at another period of history, with identical stories of abduction, mysterious objects inserted into their heads, lances or massive needles stuck into their necks and skulls, crystals implanted into their bodies, have their bones counted, their eyes and brains taken out etc.? The link is the trance state, however that state is arrived, whether through drugs, dance, sound, hypnosis, torture, or spontaneously.

In 1989, John Mack of Harvard University began to offer therapy as part of his psychiatric practice to people who believed they had been abducted by aliens. After years of case studies, Mack concluded that these encounters were not the work of aliens in spaceships from other planets. Something radical and extraordinary was happening, but Mack's instinct was that it had to do with collisions of different levels or states of reality, rather than 'nuts-and-bolts' encounters with physical human beings and equally physical aliens from an extraterrestrial planetary culture. Mack stated '*What kind of matter is the alien phenomenon? It seems to belong to that class of phenomena, not even generally accepted as existing by mainstream Western science, that seem to be* ***not of*** *this visible, known material universe and yet appear to manifest* ***in*** *it. These are phenomena….that seem to 'cross over' or to violate the radical separation of the spirit and unseen realms from the material world*'.

John Mack increasingly came to believe that the realm from which UFOs appear – and then seem to disappear back again 'between one blink of the eye and the next' – was the 'spirit world'. Graham Hancock hypothesises that 'aliens' and 'spirits' may well be the same thing, or same class of thing. As Hancock continued to investigate the parallel information between shaman experiences and alien abduction, he often wasn't sure whether he was reading a UFO abduction report or the account of a shaman's pilgrimage to the sky world. Despite surface differences appropriate to the very different cultural settings and periods in which the abductee and shamans had undergone their experiences, the clues kept mounting up that the two phenomena must be closely related at a deep structural level.

One particularly striking similarity was that, just like spirits from the shaman world, these entities that Western abductees generally construe as 'aliens' very frequently present themselves in the form of animals, or with hybrid animal and alien characteristics, before appearing in their more familiar tabloid identity as small humanoid beings with heart-shaped heads, large eyes etc., or as insect-people such as the praying mantis, as shamans have often witnessed too. Just like shaman experiences, John Mack, David Jacobs and other well-known researchers found that, in many of their hypnosis sessions, abductees revealed accounts of encounters with therianthropic aliens – strange humanoids that either had certain animal characteristics or were fully transformed into animals. Mack stated that the aliens appear to be consummate shape-shifters, often appearing to the abductees as animals – owls, eagles, raccoons and deer being among the creatures the abductees have seen initially, which replicates the experiences of shamans. Although shamans from remote tribes have never heard of aliens or UFOs abductions, they know a great deal about spirits that behave in many of the same strange ways that aliens do.

An important universal theme is the acquisition of supernatural *helpers* or *guides*, whosoever it is that accesses the 'spirit world'. Initiation often starts in childhood. It can be seen that this is replicated in alien abduction cases. The concept of the 'spirit guides' is also encountered in *The Silver Cord* (reviewed previously in Part 1) where trance-state materialisation of 'guides' from the spirit world occurred.

Whatever animal or hybrid form they appear in, and whether terrifying or friendly at first, the purpose of a shaman's spirit guides is to bestow upon him the power and teach him the requisite skills to shamanise: to travel freely and at will in the spirit world, to negotiate with its inhabitants, and to return to earth equipped to heal the sick, influence the weather, control the movements of animals, and find out the truth of hidden things – not for his own benefit but for the benefit of the tribe. UFO abductees go through the same process and regard their encounters with aliens as *important learning experiences,* which are intended to gain knowledge.

The process by which a person goes into a state of trance and enters the spirit world can be achieved through the use of hallucinogenic drugs, rhythmic dancing, 'audio-driving' (with loud repetitive drumming, etc.), sensory deprivation, self-torture, starvation and other extreme austerities. These are all amongst the techniques that shamans have used since prehistoric times to alter their consciousness and enter the spirit world.

But there have also always been shamans who have no need of any of these tried and tested 'techniques of ecstasy' because they have acquired the gift of falling spontaneously into trance. These specially gifted shamans, the spontaneous trancers, obviously provide the closest parallel to UFO abductees, whose experiences are also spontaneous and not deliberately induced. UFO abductees appear to have the built-in ability (unknown to them) to fall spontaneously into very deep states of hallucination. The findings of Rick Strassman, reported earlier, indicate that abductees spontaneously overproduce DMT from the normal levels found in the body. When this happens, in line with the actual reports of patients who ingested DMT during the Strassman sessions, alien-like and insectoid-like creatures often appeared. Subjects often reported a sexual element to their encounters, as well as knowledge-gathering.

But what would a spirit want from us? What's in it for them? It transpires from the research that there is a lot in it for them. In the short time that our different realms, physical/non-physical, come together, incredibly, often they want to mate with humans and create hybrids. The process of reproduction with essentially non-physical beings goes back to the earliest days of shamans, and has been well reported (such as the extensive research done by Jacques Vallee and detailed in *Passport to Magonia*, the encounters humans have had with fairies and, of course, the alien abduction scenario). Fairy tribes were described by the Reverend Robert Kirk in his 1691 publication *The Secret Commonwealth of the Elves, Fauns and Fairies*' as 'a distinct order of created beings possessing human-like intelligence and supernormal powers, who live and move about in this world invisible to all save men and women of the second sight'.

Although not referenced in Graham Hancock's work, another authoritative source of information on fairies, W.Y Evans Wentz's 1903 classic *The Fairy Faith in Celtic Countries* suggests that such creatures may exist. After years of study of 'fairy faith', and the gathering of hundreds of dispositions, W.Y. Evans Wentz, an authority on Eastern religions who translated *The Tibetan Book of the Dead*, stated "*we can postulate scientifically...the existence of such invisible intelligences as gods, genii, daemons, all kinds of true fairies, and disembodied man*".

Shamans, women of the 17th century, and 20th century abductees all state the same encounters, that they were taken away to strengthen the (fairy) or other races, producing hybrids and so on. Research has shown that shamans have had sex with spirits, humans have had sex and even married fairies (and disappeared sometimes) and UFO abductees have experienced what they believe is sex with aliens. The processes and procedures have changed, it seems, from the multiple reports in Hancock's book, with the alien abduction procedures undertaken being more sophisticated than those from the days of fairy abductions in the middle ages, but the project is still the same: reproduction and the strengthening of their stock.

The project has, however, evolved over the years, ironing out glitches in the abductions from the fairy days, turning the fairy dance into more efficient UFOs, relinquishing baby theft, and avoiding the late return of abductees as occurred in the past. Hancock says that, whatever name we give them - spirits, fairies, aliens - the beings have been changing and developing alongside humans for thousands of years, and cannot be simply a mass delusion, as scientists want us to believe. They must have a definite, independent reality outside the human brain.

It seems that the crux of the matter is that the non-physical forms can only hold a physical form for a very short period of time, and they want to learn how to combine solid human form and their luminous form into a more permanent, more powerful being (as reported by Thomas Bullard in his 1987 book *UFO Abductions: The Measure of a Mystery*). Hancock says that we are essentially contemplating the existence – and powerful intervention in our lives – of highly intelligent *discarnate* entities belonging to an order of creation fundamentally different from our own. Paradoxically, however, these non-physical entities seem to have mastered a 'technology' that enables them to enter our material world and to manifest in it in a quasi-physical, shape-shifting, sometimes theranthropic, sometimes large-headed and small-bodied humanoid form – but always evanescent, ephemeral, somehow luminous, almost but not quite transparent.

A reasonable explanation for all the 'spirit world' occurrences that humans have witnessed, is that 'separate, freestanding realities' or 'parallel dimensions' do exist, as Aldous Huxley, William James and Albert Hoffman have suggested. Recent television series such as *Fringe, Stranger Things, and Lost* have examined the concept of parallel dimensions in depth. These 'parallel dimensions' vibrate at a different frequency to our own and thus are invisible to us *except when we approach them in altered states of consciousness.*

These other realities seem to be inhabited by intelligent beings who are normally non-physical in our dimension and have had a long-term interest in us, interfering in and manipulating human affairs in the guise of spirit guides, supernatural teachers, fairies and, recently, aliens. Rick Strassman says (in his book *DMT: The Spirit Molecule*) that it may be that 'DMT alters the characteristics of our brains' so that we are able to perceive what the physicists call 'dark matter' – the 95 per cent of the universe's mass that is known to exist but that at present remains invisible to our senses and instruments. However, it is highly possible that these entities that reside in other dimensions can observe us even though we can't observe them, perhaps by using specific technology, techniques or their highly developed senses. Nothing should be ruled out or ridiculed.

Humanity's interest in the spirit world goes back to the start of man's consciousness 40,000 years ago when cave-painting shamans started to interact with 'spirits'. Over the millennia, in all periods of history and all parts of the world, shamans have brought back knowledge of an Otherworld, of life beyond this life, and given us guidance on living, dying, death and the afterlife through their contact in trance states with spirits, fairies, aliens and half-man half-beast or insect hybrids.

It is now understood that a trance state can be spontaneously obtained by certain humans, enabling them to interact with the spirit world, the detailed evidence of which has been reported by leading psychiatrists. The look of the 'spirits' may have changed over the millennia, and their actions and procedures when they interact with humans but, whatever form they take, it is clear that there are non-physical realms beyond our own realm, which we are sometimes lucky enough to discover while living.

APPENDIX 3

CHANGE IS COMING

Whatever you need to do, do it now. As John Lennon said: "Life is what happens to you while you are busy making other plans". Make those plans happen now. Change is coming, and we need to prepare mentally, physically and spiritually for it.

Whether we like it or not, whether we want it or not, our lives are about to change. This change is all-embracing, and will affect us mentally and physically. Various changes are imminent: Changes in the way humanity is controlled; Solar changes; Electromagnetic changes; Geo-physical changes; Spiritual changes; Changes that are man-made; Global changes in our consciousness; and an upgrade of the current human being.

Development of our immortal souls will continue unabated even though the soul's current body may perish in the coming Earth changes. Throughout this book, it can be seen that the soul is immortal and will use other bodies and other environments to continue its development.

Governments and world leaders will not warn us of a coming civilisation-ending event. The solar, electromagnetic and geophysical changes (as well as fundamental changes to the financial structures and living conditions on Earth) are predicted to be coming within a short time, well within most people's lifetime.

This will lead to a collapse of the current civilisation and large-scale destruction of the planet, but this destruction will allow an evolutionary leap of mankind to a higher stage, and enable must faster development of the soul in the next cycle of humanity.

Survival of the world we know is unlikely. We must, therefore, in these end times, gain knowledge of what is important. This involves the mind, not the body.

Spiritual changes

The coming geophysical, electromagnetic and solar changes will be explained shortly, but the most important change that is coming is spiritual.

Many people are waking up to the reality that they have been manipulated for a very long period of time, stretching back thousands of years. They are realising that the manipulation of humanity has been based on inducing fear. The methods of control through fear have remained hidden beneath the surface, and the sudden uncovering of what has been going on has been profoundly shocking. The deleting of the mind programs which have controlled humanity will take time, but the change has started.

The methods of control of humanity are set out in Appendix 4. All methods relate to attempts to block the activation of our consciousness and block the raising of our frequency. If the human frequency is raised high enough, the current Controllers on Earth can no longer control our minds. The constant process of frequency-lowering perpetrated by the Controllers produces unhappiness and discontent, as deep inside we know this is not what we incarnated to experience.

A global fence quarantine has been placed around Earth (known as HAARP, the High Altitude Aurora Resonance Project) to lower human frequencies. The Controllers are struggling to maintain this sort-of electronic dog fence, which is designed to stop the new energies coming in from the galactic plane that Earth is crossing. The Controllers have put in place multiple devices to restrain the inflow of frequency-raising energy, but are not as successful as they would wish. Their methods include HAARP, chemtrails, fluoride in the water, GMO and chemicals in the food, low frequencies emitted from TV and mobile phones amongst others.

In *A New Earth* (2005), Eckhart Tolle talks of the collapsing of the existing world order and the arising of "a new heaven and new earth" (as quoted from the Bible). This, he says, is not a location but refers to the inner realm of consciousness. "A new heaven" is the emergence of a transformed state of human consciousness, and "a new earth" is its reflection in the physical realm. Tolle goes on to say that since human life and human consciousness are intrinsically one with the life of the planet, as the old consciousness dissolves, there is bound to be synchronistic geographic and climatic natural upheavals in many parts of the planet, which we have started already to witness.

This is likely to be a pole shift, or other earth changes, and the *tabula rasa* which goes with that, the "clean slate", which will allow us to reconnect with Source.

Tolle quotes Jesus Christ: "Blessed are the poor in spirit, for theirs will be the kingdom of heaven". He interprets "poor in spirit" to mean: no inner baggage; no identifications. This is the freeing of ourselves from attachments, and the old identification with what we have, and how others view our 'worth', rather than focusing on our inner self, which is who we are. If we are 'unconscious', or lacking in awareness of what is going on around us, rather than 'conscious', we simply perpetuate the old world of greed and self-serving which is ending. A mass 'awakening' is underway now as we move to a 'new earth'. The awakening is the process of releasing our attachment to ego, our identification with possessions and image. Tolle also quotes Jesus Christ's' Sermon on the Mount where he says "Blessed are the meek for they shall inherit the Earth" - meek being the egoless people.

We saw the first awakening of global consciousness in the flower power hippie movement and the Woodstock music festival in the 1960's. The youth of that era attempted to change the status quo of society, but failed as the movement was brutally quashed. It did however bring Eastern wisdom and spirituality to the West and the focus on changing our minds, which has helped the awakening of global consciousness.

In the cycles of Earth, we have reached a point where the astrological Ages are changing, from the Age of Pisces into the Age of Aquarius. This heralds a global change of consciousness, from the Pisces concept that man must be *told* what to do by higher powers because man is incapable of thinking for himself, to the Aquarius concept or ideal that man will now *learn the truth and be able to think for himself.* This shift is significant for humanity.

There is a spiritual war being fought at this very moment between benevolent and non-benevolent forces. This is a war between those that wish to see Earth move in a spiritual (frequency-raising) direction rather than the direction it is heading at the moment which is towards materialism and atheism (frequency-lowering) and away from realisation of our divine nature and source. As more people awaken to the reality of the system of control of humanity, this will force transparency on those who prefer humanity to live in darkness, as society's apathy towards its Controllers ends.

Zbigniew Brzezinski, a powerful operator behind the scenes in the globalisation drive of the USA, wrote in 1969 an astonishing revelation which sums up the spiritual war that is going on:

"The challenge for governments in the future will be to prevent man from effectively discovering his true self. And keeping humanity locked in consumerist materialism." (Between Two Ages – Americas Role in the Techtronic Era, 1969)

This war has been going on since the earliest days of our modern civilisation, and can be traced through underground teachings all the way back to Egyptian times at least 5,000 years ago.

Knowledge: The 'Cult of Knowledge'

The idea of Light versus Dark is first seen in the Egyptian teachings set out in *The Pyramid Texts, the Coffin Texts, The Duat and The Egyptian Book of the Dead*, and then found their way into *The Hermetica,* and Gnostic literature around 2,000 years ago. These teachings were preserved underground (on account of extreme religious and governmental persecution) before appearing again 1,000 years later in Cathar, Hermetic and early Freemason writings and thinking. The underlying purpose of these teachings was to free human beings from their state of enslavement by initiating them into the 'cult of knowledge'.

The predicament of humanity, so these teachings said, was ignorance, which manifested in attachment to the vices and evils inherent in the material realm rather than the divine part of man consisting of 'mind, intellect, spirit and reason' which would allow him to ascend to the spirit realms. Knowledge was awareness of a spiritual realm of greatness 'above' which is the domain of the God of Good, the source of truth and the long-lost home of the soul. The *Hermetica*, for instance, makes statements such as "Evil, as I have told you before, must dwell here on earth, where it is at home; for the home of evil is the earth", and "You are purified, now that you have put away the earthly tabernacle".

The interest of the ancient Egyptian, Gnostic, Cathar, Bogomil, Mani, Hermetic and Rosicrucian religions, was the journey of the soul. It was seen as an immortal non-physical intelligence that entered the human body at conception and thereafter wore it like a 'tunic' (so it is said) until the body died. The soul was pictured as a time traveller on an immense journey towards perfection. The soul would need to be reborn many times in different bodies before attaining its goal. Like Buddhism, the objective was to progress to an advanced state of detachment, purity and self-control, obtainable only while in human form, that was believed necessary to release the soul forever from its imprisonment in the world of matter. The ancient Egyptian texts such as the *Duat* say as much:

A man must train his soul in this life, in order that, when it has entered the other world, where it is permitted to see God, it may not miss the way which leads to him. But men who love the body will never see the vision of the Beautiful and Good. How glorious, my son, is the beauty of that which has neither shape nor colour.

As Robert Bauval and Graham Hancock note in *The Master Game*, ancient Egyptian initiates were trained to 'see' - in other words, obtain knowledge ("*gnosis*") of what otherwise only the Gods could see. The goal was to become 'a spirit equipped for journeying', spiritually immortal and free from the fetters of matter. This beauty of the spirit realm could not be seen by uninitiated men and women because it was perceptible only to the mind and not at all to the senses.

The leaders of these secret and persecuted religions lived in such a way as to minimise spiritual pollution, living without material possessions, accepting severe austerities, fasting, vegetarianism (killing was abhorred), chastity, pacifism, and equality of the sexes. The basis of the religion was 'knowledge of the human condition': that our souls belong to (and were created by) a pure god and conversely the god that governed the material world was an evil god, the aim of the soul being to permanently escape from this material world through its conduct while inside a physical body.

Steve Taylor commented in an interview for *The Dangerous Man*, a book of conversations with free-thinkers and truth-seekers, edited by Karen Sawyer and published in 2010, that his view of history is an *anti-progressive* view – that civilisation has lost spirituality over the years. We have progressed in a technological sense, but have degenerated spiritually. The carriers of the Knowledge were crushed by the ruling powers who were threatened by knowledge of the power of the human mind and its spiritual origins.

Ari Kopel states in her book *Getting Back To Source* (2015) that many people, particularly in the New Age

Movement (to which could be added many liberal thinkers who are removed from the reality of everyday life), are in denial of the existence of evil forces who are currently in full control of this world we live in. They believe that there is no such thing as negative or evil forces, and are in denial that these forces are exerting their negative influence over humanity on a daily basis.

Additionally, people who are so-called spiritual teachers, preachers, leaders and gurus are dis-empowering us, individually, and making us think that we are not spiritually worthy to connect with God on our own. They make us think that we need some "intermediary".

We have forgotten who we are: divine souls. We are fully capable of connecting with our divine source without intermediaries, and we should never forget this. The world we live in is dis-empowering, promoting materialism over spirituality. We are mind-programmed to believe the concept that we are irrelevant specks of dust in a vast cosmos. We are told this by 'scientists' who are the new 'priesthood'. This is very persuasive in inducing us to bow down to the 'altar of materialism' as a more rewarding pursuit.

The Coming Event: Ascension

"Ascension" is a coming rare event described in Robert Monroe's 1985 book *Far Journeys* in which significant changes will occur to Earth and humankind which will not happen again for millions of years. Monroe discovered this coming event following out-of-body travels described in *Far Journeys*. Monroe said that groups of extraterrestrial beings were observing the coming Earth changes when there will be a conflux of several different and intense energy fields which will arrive at the same time within Earth's atmosphere. The arrival of this new energy will offer human consciousness the chance to emerge into a unified energy system linking with other life across the universe. Dolores Cannon also discovered this coming event which she describes in books such as *The Convoluted Universe* series (2001-12) and *The Custodians* (1998). The event was discussed at length in David Wilcock's 2016 book, *The Ascension Mysteries*, which is a good starting point to learn about the Earth changes, and is summarised below.

For many years Wilcock has been revealing information about the corruption and conspiracies going on in the world, which has given him access to certain whistle-blowers, government insiders in various secret programs, who possess knowledge of events hidden from the public. In the early 2000's, he worked with the leading exponents of whistleblower testimony, Kerry Cassidy and Bill Ryan, who ran Project Camelot, which became one of the first worldwide sensations on the newly-formed Youtube platform, revealing in particular the existence of a secret space program. Cassidy still runs Project Camelot and has helped to bring transparency to hidden affairs of the Deep State, reaching a huge worldwide audience. Her book *Rebel Gene* (2020) is an instructive read.

Wilcock reports in *The Ascension Mysteries* that the greatest secret these insiders had shared with him was that there is a massive energetic shift happening right now on Earth. He states that our solar system is apparently moving into a dense cloud of highly charged energetic particles which are now within our galaxy.

Wilcock states that insiders in the secret space program have said that spacecraft have been sent out into deep space to view this 'high-energy cloud' in order to study its energetic properties. As earth moves into this energy, the power of the energy cloud will increase to the point where it will trigger a dramatic evolutionary event on Earth. Wilcock understands from his sources that we will go through a quantum leap that changes the nature of space, time, matter, energy, consciousness, and biological life almost instantaneously.

According to Wilcock, the date range given by insiders in the secret space program for this evolutionary event is 2018 to 2023. This zone of higher energy is already having an effect on our consciousness as well as our DNA. Photons are emanating from the sun right now, which is upgrading the current human, transforming

DNA. New abilities are arising which will assist development of our souls.

Wilcock's book shows that this event is a scientific reality, which backs up the stories that appear in the Bible, the Koran, the Hindu, Mayan and Buddhist scriptures, and multiple other ancient texts that predict a time of great strife and pain on Earth that then leads to a Golden Age. This time is now.

The evidence presented by Wilcock is overwhelming, and clearly indicates that we are heading into a massive event that will transform life on Earth as we know it. It is an unavoidable event that will devastate Earth, and we need to prepare for it. All these scriptures advocate spiritual preparation for the coming event.

This is an important moment in the history of Earth, and most people are still asleep to its reality and possibilities for our souls, and are failing to prepare themselves. Taking actions which raise frequency is critical at this time. Most people ridicule anyone suggesting earth changes and the spiritual ascension that is coming, but preparation is very simple: Just follow the two pillars of what religion started out promoting – love and gratitude. In other words, helping those around us, and being aware of the consequences of our actions. Fear, stress, panic, worry and negativity are to be avoided.

The Separation

Society's controllers have effectively mind-programmed most people to ignore spirituality and fall into jealousy, materialism, aggression, and fear, and prevent us preparing effectively for this important event. Indeed, their aim is to try and stop the event as it will signal the end of their control of our souls. This has created the current war between good and evil, spirituality and materialism. Ascension will be the time of 'separation' of those who have gone down the road of materialism and those who have opted for a more spiritual outlook, the separation of those who are more concerned with service-to-self, and those whose nature and practice is that of service-to-others.

David Wilcock has obtained information from multiple government space program insiders who are aware that "arks" are used to rescue life from these events. These 'arks' were shown in the 2009 film *Knowing*, where certain chosen people were saved as a solar flare hit Earth, wiping out humanity. Wilcock says that super-advanced benevolent extraterrestrials (ET's) will support and promote life that is beneficial to the cosmos and weed out life that is harmful and destructive. For this reason they often call themselves "gardeners". Wilcock references the Bible which refers to this in the Book of Matthew with the metaphor of 'harvest'. Positive, loving people are compared to wheat, and negative, destructive entities are referred to as weeds that are allowed to grow together with the wheat – until the harvest time. Then the weeds are plucked out, one by one. The Book of Enoch, which was not included in the Bible, states that at this time, all the "wicked and godless are to be removed".

By simply looking around, it is not hard to conclude that the human race and planet Earth itself are struggling for survival at this time. Many spiritually aware people, like David Wilcock and Eckhart Tolle, are suggesting that a "new earth" is on the way. One of these spiritually aware people is the late Dolores Cannon, a well-known deep trance hypnotherapist who propounded this notion in her series of books entitled *The Convoluted Universe*.

In the hypnotherapy sessions reproduced in Volumes 2 and 3 of *The Convoluted Universe*, certain subjects spoke through their "subconscious" about the coming changes on Earth, even though the sessions were *regressive*. This was a reason why some subjects have returned to Earth, or are visiting Earth, at this time. It seems that many beings throughout the universe are watching what is occurring now on Earth and are of the view that something unique is happening. The transcripts indicate that it is the first time any planet or civilisation has gone through the events that are happening now, when an entire planet will reach the level where it will increase its frequency and vibration to allow it to shift en masse into another dimension.

In *The Convoluted Universe*, it is revealed that there is one problem with the coming dimensional shift: Not everyone currently on planet Earth will make the shift. Those that have not achieved the required vibrational frequency will remain on the old Earth. These people will not experience the peace and love that will radiate from the new Earth. They will remain on the old Earth with its wars, killing, greed, hatred, and all the other negative traits that currently make life so painful for many of the human race.

Vibrational change takes time, it cannot be done in a second, and there is little time left now before the shift is complete. Those who wish to be part of the new Earth must act now. The transcripts from the hypnotherapy sessions indicate that society will break down and the existing structures crumble. Many will not realise they have made the shift, though they may sense it.

Love and Conduct

The key to making the transition, it would seem, is that we need to operate from a standpoint of *love*. That should be our guiding motivation. *Love* is about *conduct* - how we conduct ourselves towards others. True love is shown by the way we treat others. Do we think about others as we go about our daily lives, or are we primarily self-serving? One's vibrational frequency cannot increase if we are motivated by greed, jealousy, envy, hatred, hubris, desire for control and reduction of other's free will, and the many other negative human traits that most humans still exhibit.

As Dolores Cannon writes in the New Earth section of the transcripts:

"We can change the world, one person at a time. Love is the answer, it is that simple".

If we are working for the Earth, we will be provided for. The driving force now must be love and service, not greed.

Geo-physical changes

The Coming Pole Shift

It is now scientific fact that the North Pole has changed its position four times in the last 80,000 years or so. Its position has been in the Yukon, then the Greenland Sea, then Hudson Bay and finally, to its current position, which happened around 9,600 BC. Another change is due now. Each time the North Pole moves, it causes the giant ice sheet at each pole to move thousands of miles. Formerly temperate lands freeze over because that land ends up near the North or South poles, and areas of land formerly covered in ice melt on account of that land moving into a more temperate climate. The movements are not gentle. Some movement happens so abruptly that it instantaneously freezes everything in its path. Other areas are deluged with water as ice melts.

Survival in these zones is not possible. Survival is only possible for the few people living in areas where the land remains fairly stable at the time of the shift (the pivot points). Even then, survival may be difficult unless the population in that area is well prepared. It is believed that the last pole shift took 5,000 years to fully stabilise, causing populations to continually move location to survive as weather patterns changed.

Since the end of World War II, which was the last time that the world was plunged into global chaos and millions of innocent humans died, a number of scientists have been propounding a theory that geophysical global chaos comes in cycles to Earth. This usually comes in the form of *a pole shift*, often accompanied by other Earth changes, such as a galactic superwave, which research has revealed to be imminent. Causes are explained below.

The writer most well-known for his theory of pole shift is Professor Charles Hapgood, who first wrote about the subject in his 1958 book *Earth's Shifting Crust*. Antarctica's ice cap is currently about 19 quadrillion tons and growing. Arctic ice, on the other hand, is melting. In fact, a recent NASA study (published 12 October 2018 by R Kwok of the Jet Propulsion Laboratory, California) indicates that Arctic ice is melting at a very fast rate, with Arctic ice cover losing about two-thirds of its thickness since 1958 and older ice has shrunk by nearly two million square kilometres (about 800,000 square miles). This change resembles conditions that are understood to have occurred, according to some more radical and open-minded historical researchers, at the time of the last pole shift.

Even in Antarctica though, there has been some melting in East Antarctica, and something unusual is definitely going on there. A long list of high ranking officials have been visiting areas where the snow has melted in the last few years, and reports have surfaced that evidence of past civilisations and advanced ancient technology have been revealed.

Professor Hapgood assessed that a typical pole shift creates a realignment of about thirty degrees. Scientists have stated that this shift would occur at the rate of about five or six degrees per day, so that a full pole shift would occur in about a week. Survival would be near-impossible with such rapid changes to the earth. However Hapgood didn't feel that the weight of the ice alone would be enough to set the earth in motion, but that it would also involve other factors such as a distant astronomical cause or perhaps a diminishing magnetic field on earth. The combination of these factors would overcome the friction between layers below ground (which stabilises the crust) and would cause the crust to start moving.

It seems that these 'other factors' may be in play now, in addition to the changes in the balance of ice accumulated at the poles. These other factors, being magnetic and solar events, are explained in the sections that follow. The sheer weight of the current ice accumulation at the Antarctic pole today, with most of it accumulating in West Antarctica, will weaken a critical layer of rock beneath it and end up overcoming the friction between layers in the crust which stops the earth shifting. When the moment comes that the weight is simply too much, the compressed rock layers will simply split apart, and change will happen suddenly and swiftly.

Time Magazine published an article by Hugh Auchincloss Brown shortly after the end of the Second World War entitled "Can the Earth Capsize?", which proposed that pole shifts happen at regular intervals. Brown suggested that the accumulation of ice at one or both poles eventually created significant imbalances in centrifugal forces and caused tipping of the axis by the pushing of the ice cap away from the pole and towards the equator. Brown's view was that this event occurred about every seven thousand years and that the next pole shift was due anytime. This theory formed the basis for his 1967 book *Cataclysms of the Earth*.

When a pole shift has occurred, the evidence shows that it has happened so quickly that animals which had been grazing in a previously temperate climate were literally frozen into the ice that formed suddenly, with undigested food still in their stomachs. Civilisations are crushed, deluged and exterminated so that those civilisations are reduced to myth or legend.

The coming pole shift and earth changes may well restore the rotation of Earth to its natural clockwise rotation from its current anti-clockwise rotation. Perhaps this will also restore the direction of humanity, back towards spirituality and service-to-others rather than its current direction of self-serving and materialism.

Electromagnetic changes

There have been reports from reputable sources that the Earth's magnetic poles are about to flip. When this occurs, the physical poles shift for reasons which are unclear to scientists and geologists, though some scientists believe the friction between layers below earth's crust disappears as the magnetic field weakens, causing the crust to shift. Once the magnetic field strengthens again, a few days after the initial shift, the viscosity between layers returns and the crust stabilises again (a phenomena known as "magnetohydrodynamics").

At the present time, the North Magnetic Pole is racing away from Canada and into Russia at such an accelerating pace that the United States Government has stopped allowing public access to their data. The National Oceanic and Atmospheric Administration (NOAA) recently released information that their prediction model for navigation is no longer accurate because the Magnetic North Pole is moving significantly faster than their model predicted. This World Magnetic Model, published in 2015, is already out of date. The Model tracks declination (the difference between true, or geographic, north and magnetic north) and is extremely important as it is the means by which shipping, aviation, antennas, drilling equipment and google maps (amongst other things) navigate/orientate.

In the area from Chile to Zimbabwe known as the South Atlantic Anomaly the compass which should point south *already points north*. It is believed that the authorities (such as the NOAA) already know that global magnetic pole flip is imminent and are preparing for the consequences of this event.

When we combine the above magnetic pole activity with the coming Grand Solar Minimum Big Freeze (due from the mid-2020's until the mid-2040's, which was last seen over three hundred years ago), we have the unique conditions for the occurrence of a physical pole shift. This will end this cycle of humanity.

Solar changes

Another possibility for a 'trigger' for a pole shift is a galactic superwave, the conditions for which appear to be developing now.

The astrophysicist Paul LaViolette has stated, in his 2005 book *Earth Under Fire*, that there are tremendous energetic explosions that periodically take place at the centre of galaxies (including the Milky Way galaxy, which our own solar system sits on the outer edge of) as a result of which matter and energy are spewed out (cosmic ray particles and electromagnetic emissions such as radio waves, infrared rays, light, ultraviolet rays, x-rays, and gamma rays).

This causes a wave front with an electromagnetic pulse followed by a gravity wave and light and radiation waves to spread across the galaxy. LaViolette states that it is the interstellar debris accompanying the wave, the cosmic dust, which causes the terrestrial damage, the cataclysm. The cosmic ray wind exerts so much pressure that it pushes forward interstellar dust particles which exist just outside the solar system into Earth's atmosphere. The dust collides with the Sun's magnetic field, causing friction and creating a visible static charge of plasma energy at the front end of the field that rapidly increases in size and brightness.

This appears to be happening now. An ESA/NASA project, significantly called "DUST", which was launched in 1990, has discovered that there is 300 percent more dust from our galaxy entering our solar system then there was during the 90's.

The effect of this dust and energy may be part of what has been called the "2012 Shift", which may be causing changes to our human bodies, including DNA reprogramming, increased sensitivity and intuition, changes in our materialistic outlook, and even such things as fatigue, flu-like symptoms, rashes, and other bodily sensations related to limbs, hearing, visuals and so on.

This dust or particle cloud is the possible key to the coming dramatic evolutionary event on Earth. The dust, which is already building rapidly in our atmosphere, precedes the wave.

As the wave itself reaches our solar system it becomes visible as a bright blue light, which resembles a blue eye. The centre of the gravity wave resembles the "pupil" of the eye, with a dimmer blue oval around it, as light is reflected off dust in the central bulge of the galactic disk. Paul LaViolette estimates this visible blue light lasts for about 1,000 years. At the time of first visibility it triggers a pole shift.

According to LaViolette, the galactic centre and this energy normally become visible as Earth crosses the galactic plane as it is doing now. This blue light which triggers a pole shift has been known as *the Eye of Horus* by the Egyptians, the *Blue Star Kachina* by the Hopi tribe, the *Tariq Star* by the Arabs, the *Odin Eye* by the Vikings and *Nibiru* by the Sumerians. These are just some of the names the blue light which causes devastation on Earth has been known by.

Earth and its solar system are currently crossing the galactic plane (which happens about every 25,920 years) and, while it makes this crossing, it comes into contact with the energy emitted from the galactic centre. When the winter solstice sun in the Northern Hemisphere aligns with the centre, this is often the moment for the pole shift catastrophe to occur.

LaViolette states that the last peak outburst of cosmic rays reached Earth around 12,600 years ago, based on analysis of beryllium-10 concentrations in the polar ice. During this time, unusually large quantities of acid-bearing dust were injected into the Earth's atmosphere. These cosmic ray events appear to recur in line with the duration of precessional Great Cycles. This is happening now. A flash of light given off by the Sun at the end of the cycle starts the change, the event, the cataclysm, causing geophysical and spiritual changes. This 'event' was portrayed in the 2009 film *Knowing*.

A further factor causing change is Earth's current alignment with the sun's companion star, which occurs every 25,000 years according to masonic and Mayan researchers. This invisible brown dwarf star has been called Nibiru. During this alignment the Earth gets a huge energy surge. The sun's alleged companion star is, of course, not widely known, or discussed, in the mainstream media.

Finally, there is another solar event which could also trigger a pole shift. This is a coronal mass ejection (commonly known as a "CME").

NASA takes this possibility seriously. On 26th October 2006 NASA launched the Solar Terrestrial Relations Observatory (known as Stereo) which consists of two near identical spacecraft which produce stereoscopic images of CME's and other solar activity measurements. By October 2010, the spacecraft were almost diametrically opposite each other in orbit, giving the best possible readings for any coming catastrophe. This will allow some warning of when and where a massive CME might hit the earth, as such an event will cause devastation to those above ground level.

A point of stability is at the centre of earth's land mass, which is where the pyramids were built. After the last destruction, civilisation first rose up again in the middle eastern area, as this was one of the most stable locations at that time, and was occupied by survivors from the pole shift. Whilst all of the earth rotated, the central areas, those areas that experience minimal changes in latitude or elevation (the pivot points) would not have witnessed rotation like the large change in latitude of areas near the poles such as Siberia and Antarctica. Many areas designated by sacred sites also fit into this 'stable earth' category at the time of an earth crust slippage.

Changes caused by Humanity

At the time of writing in late-2020, it has become clear that the actions of the population of Earth are causing changes to the planet, which now includes a virus pandemic that caused Governments to force most of the global population to stay at home as a method of fighting the virus. The virus and the ensuing "forced lockdown" has had hugely damaging consequences for humanity.

Viruses are not new to the planet. As Richard Preston shows in his 1994 book *The Hot Zone*, one of the most frightening books ever written, the decimation of the rain forests of Africa has unleashed on the world a wave of deadly viruses on its human invaders, such as HIV, Marburg and Ebola. And, greed and profit was at the heart of the invasion of the rain forests. Occasionally, these viruses leak out from the laboratories where they are being studied.

According to Preston, the emerging viruses are surfacing from ecologically damaged parts of the earth. The earth is beginning to react to the "human parasite, the flooding infection of people, the dead spots of concrete all over the planet, the cancerous rot outs in Europe, Japan and the United States, thick with replicating primates, the colonies enlarging and spreading and threatening to shock the biosphere with mass extinctions." Preston goes on to state that nature has interesting ways of balancing itself. The rain forests (from where the viruses emerge) have their own defences. He says "The earth's immune system is seeing the presence of the human species and is starting to kick in. The earth is attempting to rid itself of an infection by the human parasite".

Chemical pollution of water and soil are further hazards which will decimate humanity. Desert zones and infertile lands are increasing. Seas have dead zones now. The end appears to be nigh. And who loses and who wins from the greed and destruction? As Thom Hartmann says in his 1999 book *The Last Hours of Ancient Sunlight*:

Around the world we find that rapid growth is straining virtually all nations, and the greatest pain is usually experienced by the individual people and families who do not share the extreme power and wealth of the society's ruling elite (whether the elite is corporate, governmental or military).

Although Hartmann's book was written two decades ago, it clearly shows how humanity is getting close to wiping itself out by the drive for profit and greed as critical resources required for our survival (such as trees for oxygen, drinking water and so on) are depleted. Hartmann's book can be seen as a "wake up call" to the world. It is about waking up to the complete destruction of the planet. The majority of humanity seem to be completely unaware about the on-going destruction of the planet, a lack of caring, wanton greed, and service-to-self only.

Key features discussed by Hartmann are overpopulation, depletion of resources, pollution and toxic air, the combined effects of which cause planetary destruction. When resources get sparse, bad things happen: disease, war, starvation, horrible death. The citizens of the richer Western nations believe they are immune from the world's hot spots, the horrors of Haiti, parts of Africa, and so on. But, in the end, it gets us all.

Additionally, the air is becoming more and more toxic. The rainforests are being cut down at a fast rate, and they largely provide the oxygen needed to keep humanity alive. Large areas of rainforests are being cut down to satisfy corporate greed and provide cheap grazing for cattle that are butchered and exported to provide beef for cheap burgers in the West. Water is also becoming undrinkable in many parts of the world due to contamination of groundwater. Empires decline when they can't get access to resources; war becomes inevitable in these circumstances.

We need to make huge changes in the way we see and understand the world and recognise the need to control our population, save our forests, reduce wasteful consumption and re-create community. We can be of the opinion that we are helpless to stop the inevitable end and choose to escape from harsh reality into mindless television, drug addiction and the like. Or, we can (as Hartmann recommends) take steps such as downsizing, moving to the country and becoming self-sustaining, accepting the concept of "enough", sharing, living in community. Unfortunately, that more-balanced world is likely to come about only after total planetary breakdown.

Cycles and Predictions

A cycle of time ended on 21st December 2012. The Hopis, the Mayans, the Maoris, the Zulus, the Hindus, the Incas, the Aztecs, the Dogons, the Pueblos, the Cherokees, the Tibetan Kalachakras, the ancient Egyptian Great Pyramid stone calendar, Nostradamus, the Bible Code, the celebrated American psychic Edgar Cayce, numerous crop circles and many 'channeled' sources such as Dolores Cannon attest to this. All predicted that global change would occur following the end of this time cycle.

On David Wilcock's website, divinecosmos.com, he references Francois Masson's book *The End of our Century* and transcribes in full a chapter entitled *Cyclology – The Mathematics of History.* Masson shows us that the cosmic clock has a divine number of 25920, which repeats itself continually, causing change at the end of every cosmic cycle (of years). Within the divine cycle are smaller cycles where change also occurs. These include the cycle of 2160 years corresponding to the precessional passage from one constellation of the Zodiac to the next, the cycles of civilisation which correspond to the Biblical cycle of 7x77 years (539), and the basic human cycle which is 11 years and 11x7 (77) which are the cycles of Man. Wilcock shows that within these smaller cycles, events appear to repeat themselves.

As Paul LaViolette says in *Earth Under Fire*, the ice core beryllium-10 record indicates that galactic superwaves pass Earth about once every 25,000 years or so, approximating the period of one polar precessional cycle.

LaViolette has talked of a "superwave prophesy" relating to the coming Earth changes made by a Bulgarian mystic, Peter Deunov, who had a vision just days before his death in December 1944. He prophesied the onset of a superwave which he said would purify the Earth in the near future, causing both geological transformation and spiritual changes to the Earth. This superwave would bring into being a new human race, which he called "the sixth race". His detail concerning the effects of the superwave is extraordinary bearing in mind his vision was made in 1944, before much was known about active galaxies and galactic core explosions.

The English translation is so remarkable that it is reproduced in its entirety below. The lengthy prophecy stated as follows:

"During the passage of time, the consciousness of man traversed a very long period of obscurity. This phase which the Hindus call 'Kali Yuga', is on the verge of ending. We find ourselves today at the frontier between two epochs: that of Kali Yuga and that of the New Era that we are entering.

A gradual improvement is already occurring in the thoughts, sentiments and acts of humans, but everybody will soon be subjugated to divine Fire, that will purify and prepare them in regards to the New Era. Thus man will raise himself to a superior degree of consciousness, indispensable to his entrance to the New Life. That is what one understands by 'Ascension'.

Some decades will pass before this Fire will come, that will transform the world by bringing it a new moral. This immense wave comes from cosmic space and will inundate the entire earth. All those that attempt to oppose it will be carried off and transferred elsewhere.

Although the inhabitants of this planet do not all find themselves at the same degree of evolution, the new wave will be felt by each one of us. And this transformation will not only touch the Earth, but the ensemble of the entire Cosmos.

The best and only thing that man can do now is to turn towards God and improve himself consciously, to elevate his vibratory level, so as to find himself in harmony with the powerful wave that will soon submerge him.

The Fire of which I speak, that accompanies the new conditions offered to our planet, will rejuvenate, purify, reconstruct everything: the matter will be refined, your hearts will be liberated from anguish, troubles, incertitude, and they will become luminous; everything will be improved, elevated; the thoughts, sentiments and negative acts will be consumed and destroyed.

Your present life is a slavery, a heavy prison. Understand your situation and liberate yourself from it. I tell you this: exit from your prison! It is really sorry to see so much misleading, so much suffering, so much incapacity to understand where one's true happiness lies.

Everything that is around you will soon collapse and disappear. Nothing will be left of this civilization nor its perversity; the entire earth will be shaken and no trace will be left of this erroneous culture that maintains men under the yoke of ignorance. Earthquakes are not only mechanical phenomena, their goal is also to awaken the intellect and the heart of humans, so that they liberate themselves from their errors and their follies and that they understand that they are not the only ones in the universe.

Our solar system is now traversing a region of the Cosmos where a constellation that was destroyed left its mark, its dust. This crossing of a contaminated space is a source of poisoning, not only for the inhabitants of the earth, but for all the inhabitants of the other planets of our galaxy. Only the suns are not affected by the influence of this hostile environment. This region is called "the thirteenth zone"; one also calls it "the zone of contradictions". Our planet was enclosed in this region for thousands of years, but finally we are approaching the exit of this space of darkness and we are on the point of attaining a more spiritual region, where more evolved beings live.

The earth is now following an ascending movement and everyone should force themselves to harmonize with the currents of the ascension. Those who refuse to subjugate themselves to this orientation will lose the advantage of good conditions that are offered in the future to elevate themselves. They will remain behind in evolution and must wait tens of millions of years for the coming of a new ascending wave.

The earth, the solar system, the universe, all are being put in a new direction under the impulsion of Love. Most of you still consider Love as a derisory force, but in reality, it is the greatest of all forces! Money and power continue to be venerated as if the course of your life depended upon it. In the future, all will be subjugated to Love and all will serve it. But it is through suffering and difficulties that the consciousness of man will be awakened.

The terrible predictions of the prophet Daniel written in the bible relate to the epoch that is opening. There will be floods, hurricanes, gigantic fires and earthquakes that will sweep away everything. Blood will flow in abundance. There will be revolutions; terrible explosions will resound in numerous regions of the earth. There where there is earth, water will come, and there where there is water, earth will come. God is Love; yet we are dealing here with a chastisement, a reply by Nature against the crimes perpetrated by man since the night of time against his Mother; the Earth.

After these sufferings, those that will be saved, the few, will know the Golden Age, harmony and unlimited beauty. Thus keep your peace and your faith when the time comes for suffering and terror, because it is written that not a hair will fall from the head of the just. Don't be discouraged, simply follow your work of personal perfection.

You have no idea of the grandiose future that awaits you. A New Earth will soon see day. In a few decades the work will be less exacting, and each one will have the time to consecrate spiritual, intellectual and artistic activities. The question of rapport between man and woman will be finally resolved in harmony; each one having the possibility of following their aspirations. The relations of couples will be founded on reciprocal respect and esteem. Humans will voyage through the different planes of space and breakthrough intergalactic space. They will study their functioning and will rapidly be able to know the Divine World, to fusion with the Head of the Universe.

The New Era is that of the sixth race. Your predestination is to prepare yourself for it, to welcome it and to live it. The sixth race will build itself around the idea of Fraternity. There will be no more conflicts of personal interests; the single aspiration of each one will be to conform himself to the Law of Love. The sixth race will be that of Love. A new continent will be formed for it. It will emerge from the Pacific, so that the Most High can finally establish His place on this planet.

The founders of this new civilization, I call them 'Brothers of Humanity' or also 'Children of Love'. They will be unshakeable for the good and they will represent a new type of men. Men will form a family, as a large body, and each people will represent an organ in this body. In the new race, Love will manifest in such a perfect manner, that today's man can only have a very vague idea.

The earth will remain a terrain favourable to struggle, but the forces of darkness will retreat and the earth will be liberated from them. Humans seeing that there is no other path will engage themselves to the path of the New Life, that of salvation. In their senseless pride, some will, to the end hope to continue on earth a life that the Divine Order condemns, but each one will finish by understanding that the direction of the world doesn't belong to them.

A new culture will see the light of day, it will rest on three principal foundations: the elevation of woman, the elevation of the meek and humble, and the protection of the rights of man.

The light, the good, and justice will triumph; it is just a question of time. The religions should be purified. Each contains a particle of the Teaching of the Masters of Light, but obscured by the incessant supply of human deviation. All the believers will have to unite and to put themselves in agreement with one principal, that of placing Love as the base of all belief, whatever it may be. Love and Fraternity that is the common base! The earth will soon be swept by extraordinary rapid waves of Cosmic Electricity. A few decades from now beings who are bad and lead others astray will not be able to support their intensity. They will thus be absorbed by Cosmic Fire that will consume the bad that they possess. Then they will repent because it is written that "each flesh shall glorify God".

Our mother, the earth, will get rid of men that don't accept the New Life. She will reject them like damaged fruit. They will soon not be able to reincarnate on this planet; criminals included. Only those that possess Love in them will remain.

There is not any place on earth that is not dirtied with human or animal blood; she must therefore submit to a purification. And it is for this that certain continents will be immersed while others will surface. Men do not suspect to what dangers they are menaced by. They continue to pursue futile objectives and to seek pleasure. On the contrary those of the sixth race will be conscious of the dignity of their role and respectful of each one's liberty. They will nourish themselves exclusively from products of the vegetal realm. Their ideas will have the power to circulate freely as the air and light of our days.

The words "If you are not born again" apply to the sixth race. Read Chapter 60 of Isaiah it relates to the coming of the sixth race, the Race of Love.

After the Tribulations, men will cease to sin and will find again the path of virtue. The climate of our planet will be moderated everywhere and brutal variations will no longer exist. The air will once again become pure, the same for water. The parasites will disappear. Men will remember their previous incarnations and they will feel the pleasure of noticing that they are finally liberated from their previous condition.

In the same manner that one gets rid of the parasites and dead leaves on the vine, so act the evolved Beings to prepare men to serve the God of Love. They give to them good conditions to grow and to develop themselves, and to those that want to listen to them, they say: "Do not be afraid! Still a little more time and everything will be all right; you are on the good path. May he that wants to enter in the New Culture study, consciously work and prepare."

Thanks to the idea of Fraternity, the earth will become a blessed place, and that will not wait. But before, great sufferings will be sent to awaken the consciousness. Sins accumulated for thousands of years must be redeemed. The ardent wave emanating from On High will contribute in liquidating the karma of peoples. The liberation can no longer be postponed. Humanity must prepare itself for great trials that are inescapable and are coming to bring an end to egoism.

Under the earth, something extraordinary is preparing itself. A revolution that is grandiose and completely inconceivable will manifest itself soon in nature. God has decided to redress the earth, and He will do it! It is the end of an epoch; a new order will substitute the old, an order in which Love will reign on earth."

We have now reached the end of a cosmic cycle (25920 years), which brings an era to a close and presages, or augurs, change on earth. Change needs to come; earth is screaming out for it.

Change is certainly coming. The third of the three 1917 prophesies/visions in Fatima, Portugal, by three young cousins, has never been revealed but it is likely related to the end of the world as we know it. The Vatican refused, in 1960, to reveal the third vision as it was 'too horrible', though in 1984 Pope Benedict (as Cardinal Ratzinger) elaborated by stating they corresponded to 'what Scripture announces' and were 'perils that threaten humanity'. Pope John Paul II went further when speaking in Fulda, Germany when he stated:

It should be sufficient for all Christians to know this: if there is a message in which it is written that the oceans will flood whole areas of the earth, and that from one moment to the next millions of people will perish, truly the publication of such a message is no longer something to be so much desired.

The Event

Sometime between 21 December 2019 and the end of October 2029.

In the August-September 2018 edition of the excellent alternative news magazine *Nexus* it was reported, at the Secret History of Australia Conference held in Brisbane in June 2018, that a number of Aboriginal people have felt, heard or experienced some sort of vision or message regarding dramatic events to occur in the coming next few years from the time of the Conference.

The messages being received indicate that there is to be a massive shift of frequencies, energy and consciousness, along with a lot of physical changes. A growing number of Elders within the Aboriginal Community are speaking of the coming changes, the "End of Days", and are preparing themselves for the coming changes.

These visions and messages need to be taken seriously as the Aboriginal culture has seen it all before, being the culture that has been on the planet longest and with the most continuity of experience and knowledge passed down from generation to generation. Books such as Bruce Chatwin's *The Songlines* (1989) and Margo Morgan's *Mutant Message Down Under* (1990) testify to the deep knowledge of this planet possessed by the Aboriginal people.

In the August-September issue of *Nexus*, the Editor, Duncan Roads, interviewed Trent Lynwood, an Australian with Aboriginal heritage, who received a message that an energy wave is coming and that we need to "stop what we are doing and get ready as a big change is coming on Earth" within the next two years (he believed this would be in December 2019 or not long thereafter) and we all need to mentally and physically prepare for this coming change. Humanity will change drastically as both geophysical and spiritual changes occur.

Some commentators have said that the Book of Revelation's "Great Sign in Heaven" which begins the seven years of Tribulation occurred on 23 September 2017, leading up to a pole shift in 2024. (See an article in wakingtimes.com on 31 October 2018 entitled *Pole Shift, Prophesies and Ascension – the Coming War and the Future of Humanity*).

Dolores Cannon said that Nostradamus had predicted a pole shift in October 2029. David Wilcock in his book *The Ascension Mysteries* (referenced earlier) says from his insider information that the time frame for change is 2018-2023.

In David Montaigne's book *End Times and 2019*, subtitled *The End of the Mayan Calendar and the Countdown to Judgment Day,* he calculates that the date for the start of global geophysical changes on Earth is seven years after the end of the Mayan calendar and the winter solstice of 21 December 2012. This is the time of a planetary alignment of Venus, Mars, Mercury, and Jupiter, as well as the winter solstice sun being in alignment with the galactic centre, as stated in the Dresden Codex of the Mayan *Popul Vuh* depicting the time of the end of the world. This occurs in 2019, not 2012.

According to Montaigne therefore, this makes the date for an event such as a pole shift anytime from *21 December 2019*. As can be seen in this section, there are multiple predictions and prophesies, but they all come within the time frame of 2019-2029.

Montaigne references a 1926 occult book *Mystery of the Cathedrals*, written under a pseudonym "Fulcanelli", which explains that cosmic disasters happen in predictable cycles. This book referred to a stone monument at Hendaye on the border between France and Spain which warns of a cyclic catastrophe at the time when the solstices cross the galactic axis. In other words, now.

At the end of each precessional cycle, which occurs about every 25-26,000 years, an event of destruction appears to occur. There is scientific evidence, reported by David Montaigne in his book *End Times and 2019*, that Neanderthals nearly died out around 50,000 years ago when that variety was almost extinguished, and then 25,000 years later, the Neanderthal was actually extinguished.

In Karen Sawyer's book of interviews with free-thinkers and truth-seekers, *A Dangerous Man*, David Icke said that whenever he thinks of the universe, he thinks of a donut-shape going round and round. Cycles repeat themselves, which for Earth is approximately every 26,000 years in line with the precession of the equinoxes. At the end of each cycle, the planet moves into alignment with a massive energy beam, sometimes called the 'photon belt', rebalancing and realigning anything which is out of balance. As we go through it, with all the rebalancing and realigning, we come out on the other side of the photon belt into the start of a new era, a 'New Age'. This is the time for that change.

APPENDIX 4

CONTROL OF HUMANITY

It is becoming increasingly apparent to any "awake and aware" person that society is majorly controlled. Negative influence and agendas prevail, which attempt to bring unhappiness and misery to humanity as part of the effort to control Earth's large population. In order to combat this negativity, we must first understand it. Once we understand the methods of control, we can use our mental and spiritual power to step beyond the system of control.

A feature of the control system is the inducement of fear, which lowers the human body's vibration into the range where that body can be easily controlled. As the vibration of the body is raised, which is achieved through understanding what is going on, as knowledge combats fear, the methods of control become ineffective. We need to rediscover our true spiritual being and essence as this also releases fear. This is the primary premise of this book: realising our true spiritual nature.

All control methods outlined below will limit soul development. Item 16, transhumanism, which is the direction humanity's Controllers wish to take us, may even tamper with the soul's purity.

So, how is control of society achieved? The key methods of control are summarised below:

1. ***Breed conflict.*** Breeding conflict between people can be a very effective tool for maintaining social and political control over a group of people. The technique, made famous by Machiavelli, is to (a) create conflicts and issues which will cause people to fight amongst themselves rather than against the perpetrator (b) remain hidden from view as the true instigator of the conflicts (c) lend support to all sides of the conflict and (d) be viewed as the benevolent source which can solve the conflicts even though you are the guilty party.

   As William Bramley pointed out in his 1989 book *The Gods of Eden* (which was far ahead of its time though many have since added to and updated his analysis of how society is controlled), the requirement to stay out of sight was achieved by the creation of secret societies, a far-flung network of politically powerful organizations that could create conflict secretly. The Controllers of humanity used the secret societies to breed war between humans. This still goes on today. Wars are a perfect tool for making physical survival on Earth an all-consuming chore, because they absorb large-scale resources and offer little to enhance life in return. The idea is to destroy what has been created so that humans are required to start from nothing again. Fighting must be kept artificially alive by creating unresolvable 'issues' that can only be settled by the complete annihilation of one side – and then ensuring this doesn't happen by equalising their fighting strengths. So-called friendly Governments do this all the time.

2. ***Religious control.*** Doctrines of fear are very much part of today's religions. Most religions promote the idea that we must follow specific rules or else we will not become one of the 'chosen ones', whatever that is, and would end up in some hell-like place for eternity. This was, and still is, a hugely effective tool for creating fear, control, obedience and misery and at the same time creating funding, as people were required to donate funds to ensure a better life, and exoneration from past sins to ensure avoidance of hell. These forms of indoctrination ensured people would tolerate, and even welcome, unremitting physical hardship, conflict and death.

   Religious texts and leaders even encouraged the faithful to go out and attack those who held different beliefs. This would ensure eternal salvation. Each religion proclaims it is the only true religion, thus setting in motion more senseless conflict between the believers and non-believers. Religious wars have blighted Earth for millennia and still do. Religious and spiritual doctrines which exalt combat are doctrines which degrade the human race. Violence should have no place in society. The hunting down of heretics, the use of torture such as during the time of the Inquisition, and the warnings against 'false prophets' has led to some of the most bloody fighting between Hebrews, Christians and Muslims.

   The hangover from the burning and torture which was inflicted on people for centuries for disbelief in a particular religion is still visible today in the instinctive fear people have in expressing any kind of non-conforming idea. This is 'Controller mind-control' of the highest order. For a detailed analysis of why religion is harmful, one need look no further than Christopher Hitchens' 2007 bestselling paperback *God is not Great*, which has the subtext "how religion poisons everything". Chapter Two, entitled *Religion Kills*, says it all.

3. *Fear.* The lowest level of vibratory state of the human body is the state of fear. Fear is a desirable state as far as the Controllers are concerned, as control of that human is significantly easier. Spiritual awareness, where the human body has a high vibration, reducing fear, makes control more difficult.

   Dr John B. Watson, a pioneer researcher in human behaviour at John Hopkins University observed that new-born babies had no fear of the dark, no fear of animals, or noises and so on, but he discovered that babies could easily be *made* to fear *anything*. You simply condition them to fear. Through his experiments, Watson formulated a pivotal theory that was one of the foundations of 20th century social and cultural engineering: he claimed that the primary motivator for human beings is fear. In other words, if you want a human being to do or not do something, scare them. We need to be made to obey. Hence, behavioural engineering was born.

   The Jesuits, under the direction of their founder, Ignatius Loyola, were the first group to express the view that you can mould a person's mind if you can capture them in their first seven years of life. Modern techniques to create fear have significantly extended the original techniques of the Jesuits.

4. ***Disease.*** Many diseases, and in particular recent virus spreading such as SARS, MERS, AIDS, and Covid-19 are likely to be man-made. They create great suffering and conflict. If life starts to progress too successfully for the masses, a wide spread plague will successfully bring this to a halt if a war hasn't. Governments today can spread disease easily if they so desire; they have stock piles of viruses readily available.

5. ***The monetary system.*** The creation of today's monetary system, which lends itself to economic hardship through debt and inflation, remains a vital tool for the rulers of society. Governments created the modern money system for a simple reason: It enables them to fight and prolong wars, and control society. Banks have the legal right to create money out of thin air, backed by nothing, and then lend that not-in-existence money to someone against security of a real asset. Mostly they don't even bother to print the paper. But either way it creates debt and an increasingly valueless currency. Of course, should the debtor fail to pay, the real asset owned by the debtor is taken in as compensation. This is easy to manipulate, because the rulers control the money supply anyway. The struggle of the average human for survival in a modern economy where debt creation, erosion of the value of people's money, and taxation constantly take their toll, is exactly what society's controllers desire. Debt is a fundamental tool in the control of society.

   A tool increasingly used by society's controllers to define what sort of person the Controllers have to take account of and whether they are a threat, is a feature called the "cashless society". The "cashless society" is a cashless system for payments, which is being rapidly introduced, especially through the cover plan of 'viruses' which the authorities say can be easily transmitted via paper transactions (which cannot be tracked by the Controllers of course, and are therefore not desirable). The "cashless society" is an accurate and non-intrusive data surveillance system which reveals a total picture about the spending and purchasing history of a person. A person's political, sexual and religious persuasions are easily deduced, as are any activities considered illegal by the governing authorities. When this is combined with the revelations about a person's life available from the monitoring of a person's internet activities, a total picture of a person's life can be obtained. This is where society is heading now – into mass surveillance.

6. ***Codex Alimentarius.*** This is the establishment of global legislation for the supply of food. The pharmaceutical industry is attempting to re-classify any food which has a medicinal benefit as a drug. The legislation is geared towards the removal of personal freedom and choice. The political objective behind this global legislation is about absolute control. Henry Kissinger said in 1992: "Control the oil and you control nations; control the food and you control the people".

7. ***Rules and Regulations.*** Happiness can be easily and effectively reduced through rules and

regulations, either through religious laws or state laws. Many religions and nations actively forbid alcohol, gambling, dancing and singing, and limit sexual pleasure, and other forms of entertainment used by humans to create happiness in their lives. Religions, for instance, have expounded the idea that "a man at ease was a man lost". Happiness and enjoyment are not desirable features when setting up a system of control. The introduction of a 'virus' into society gives Governments the excuse for new regulations to restrict freedom.

8. ***Political doctrines.*** A classic conflict was created by the arrival of communism versus capitalism. These opposing philosophies produced the half-century long "Cold War" and much suffering. The idea of 'good' political doctrines fighting 'bad' political doctrines produces inevitable conflicts. Communism for instance was an extraordinary concept where everyone was supposedly equal and encouraged its citizens to accept conditions of social repression and dictatorship. This does not lend itself to happiness. The German Nazi experience created a vicious world war, extraordinary ignorance and obedience to a dictator, based on doctrines of 'good' and 'evil', mass exterminations, and it all happened within a time period that many can remember.

9. ***Media mind programming.*** The mass population have long been served a diet of only what the mass media desire you to hear. A small number of elite individuals and corporations control the media

outlets, and therefore both the content of the program you watch on television ('programming') and the use of subliminal imagery ensure control over our thought processes. This has been excellently portrayed in long-ago movies such as John Carpenter's 1988 'science fiction' masterpiece *They Live*, Sidney Lumet's 1976 classic *Network*. Sometimes movies reveal more than words can.

10. ***Self-Regulation.*** Media mind programming leads to the natural process of self-regulation by the masses of themselves. This saves humanity's Controllers a lot of time and effort. The elite manipulate the "herd", largely using the herd itself to police one another, ridicule and condemnation being a standard tool for those with a different spin on life.

    People generally fear what others think of them, and this regulates almost everyone, we are conditioned by what our parents, family, friends, work colleagues and so on think. This method of control is sometimes called 'political correctness'. It is largely used nowadays by bullies to win losing arguments or suppress opposing ideas or arguments. It is an easy way to silence someone, as most people do not wish to be considered outside society's self-imposed rules. If a bully is losing an argument, all that bully has to do is accuse the other person of racism, homophobia, anti-semitism or sexism. Victory and silence is assured. The films *Good Night, and Good Luck (2005)* and *The Majestic (2001)* are good examples of films which show the combating of bullying, whether such bullying is perpetrated by the State itself or by herd opinion.

In David Icke's *Tales from the Time Loop*, he summarises the method of self-regulation as follows:

It starts with conditioned parents who impose their conditioning on children and pressure them to follow their religious, political, economic and cultural norms. There are not enough of the manipulators and their stooges to control the population physically and they have to create a structure in which humans control themselves through mental, emotional, and increasingly, physical imposition.

11. ***Centralisation.*** According to David Icke in his *Guide to the Global Conspiracy*, a voluminous and persuasive book written in 2007 which is now a leading text on this subject, the classic operating method of elite control involves a requirement that there is little regard or emotion relating to the mass of the population; they are there solely to carry out functions required by the rulers.

    To ensure control is absolute, their methods require the suppression of any individuality or spirit. And increasingly, the world envisaged by George Orwell in *1984,* his classic work on totalitarianism, is coming to pass. The knowledge of how to free oneself from mental and physical control has been systematically suppressed. Surveillance of every aspect of our lives by the State is complete and absolute. We must free ourselves from Orwell's vision of the future: "imagine a boot stamping on a human face – forever".

So how does the control system work? As David Icke says, when you are just a few people compared with the vast labour force you need to control, the critical feature must be centralised decision-making. You simply can't have decisions relating to policy on control and power taken anywhere other than at the top table. And the process of centralisation has now effectively covered all areas of human life.

Centralisation is achieved through what Icke calls the "pyramid of manipulation". He says:

The same compartmentalisation of knowledge used by the secret societies is repeated in the structure of government, banking, business and every other organisation and institution. Only a few at the top of the 'individual' pyramids know the real agenda and what the organisation is trying to achieve. The further you go down the pyramid, the more people are involved in the organisation, but the less they know about the real agenda. They are only aware of the job they do every day. They don't know how their contribution connects with those other employees in other areas of the company, government or whatever. They are 'compartmentalised' and the only people who know how it all fits together are at the top. Through the pyramid within pyramid structure, the elite families can coordinate the same policies through apparently unconnected, even 'opposing', areas of society. All roads lead eventually to them, - everything from the food we eat, the water we drink, the medical care we receive, the news we watch, hear and read, the entertainment we are given, the governments that dictate to us, the military who enforce the wills of the governments."

12. ***Problem-Reaction-Solution.*** A well-known method of changing society into the direction the controllers wish it to proceed is through the method called "Problem-Reaction-Solution". The process of control can be speeded up by what Icke calls the process of "Problem-Reaction-Solution." It is utilised to bring about changes that might otherwise be resisted by the mass of the population.

    Firstly one has to create a *problem* while blaming someone else, then create a public *reaction* of fear, outrage, and general demands from the people that 'something must be done', and then it allows a *solution* to be introduced by those in power which entails changes in society which restrict freedoms, but are deemed 'necessary' and accepted by the people for their safety. The more outrageous and traumatising the event that is utilised to create the problem, the easier it is for governments to take away our freedoms under the guise of our safety and security.

13. ***Technology.*** Modern technology is now a primary method of control. Virtually all the mind-control comes from consumer-level technologies, products, and services which people happily pay for and use. The tools of humanity's slavery have been hidden in plain sight, in all the things people desire, which is always the last place they look. This programming is delivered via psychotronic technology hidden within consumer technology, namely televisions, computer monitors and cell phones. The controllers can listen to us through the devices we use.

    It is about monitoring the general public's overall

level of awareness/awakeness, so that they can adapt their agenda and identify potential "trouble-makers", those who might be waking up. The idea is to ensure lower frequency of the human body. In addition to the mind control aspect, cell/mobile phones allow them to monitor people wherever they go, not just in the home or workplace. Any device with a screen is likely to have this capability. The only difference between *1984* and the real world in this regard is that in *1984* the characters knew they were being watched.

14. ***"Dumbing Down" of the population.*** The education system for the masses has long been designed to reduce the level of awareness and intelligence. The air, water and food is chemically affected to reduce awareness and increase the ability to control. Chemicals are being sprayed into the air ("chem-trails"), fluoride has been introduced to most water sources, food now includes toxins like MSG and Aspartame, there is EM-psychotronic radiation from televisions, computers, wi-fi, cell/mobile phones and towers, drugs are prescribed to pacify us, and subliminals are used in television programming and games. All of these are about reducing human consciousness.

15. ***The "Scientific Priesthood".*** In areas such as food, air, water, space travel and the cosmos (in other words, things that are fundamental to our lives) we are told to bow down to some kind of scientific priesthood whose knowledge and opinions should never be questioned. In reality, rich and powerful

corporations and individuals have manipulated what is termed "science" and have been able, through their power and influence, to distort scientific research. The public is programmed never to question the opinions of 'scientists'.

16. ***The Transhumanist Agenda.*** This is the 'end game' of the Controllers. This is the merger of man with machine - the transformation of the human body through its enhancement with artificial intelligence, allowing Society's Controllers to control that body from a central control system. In theory, transhumanism appears to benefit the human race, allowing it to evolve beyond its current physical and mental limitations, but where control over the functions of that body can be exercised by someone other than the person themselves, benefits may be an illusion.

Most people are likely to be unwilling to cede control over their body to an unknown and unaccountable person or corporation, and this is where Item 12 above (Problem-Reaction-Solution) comes in useful. Change in attitude can be achieved through a crisis to accelerate the agenda. The Covid-19 crisis achieves this goal.

The control of humanity through a central computer system has long been desired by the Controllers. This removes the need to concern themselves with all the much more problematic methods to control humanity mentioned in Items 1-15 earlier in this Appendix 4.

How can this goal be achieved? The method is set out in plain sight for everyone who is aware and looking. The technology has finally reached the point where the goal of this agenda can be realised, and in 2010, the Rockefeller Foundation released a paper entitled *Scenarios for the Future of Technology and International Development*, better known as "the lockstep document". This document details the steps to be taken for a world of tighter top-down control and more authoritarian leadership to combat citizen dissent.

The "lockstep" was able to be activated after the Covid-19 "pandemic" surfaced in Western countries at the beginning of 2020. In June 2020, with Covid-19 having caused a shutdown of most economies and country borders for the previous six months, the solution to the crisis was announced by the World Economic Forum (an elite membership of the world's richest industrial leaders, based in Geneva, Switzerland) and was called "The Great Re-set". This re-set plan follows the blueprint already formulated.

The Great Re-set brings forward the long-standing agenda for global governance promoted by the United Nations in their *2030 UN Agenda for Sustainable Development*. The World Economic Forum (WEF) website states:

One silver lining of the pandemic is that it has shown how quickly we can make radical changes to our lifestyles. We must use it to secure the Great Re-set that we so badly need.

The Re-set is the transhumanist agenda. A WEF video published in 2017 discusses "The Fourth Industrial Revolution" stating (amongst other things): "the idea of the 'human' being a 'natural' concept is really going to change, our bodies will be so high tech we won't be able to distinguish between what is natural and what is artificial". The "Fourth Industrial Revolution" is AI (artificial intelligence).

The merger of natural and artificial in the human body will lead to the ability to access, control and manipulate people's thoughts, as well as speech and movement. This is stated in clear language on the WEF website. The Covid-19 crisis will allow destruction of the existing control system and the ushering in of a new control system.

The new control system will involve a now-attainable technology change: the implanting of radio-frequency identity (RFID) chips inside all humans, via an immunisation (vaccination) program. The RFID chips will be linked to the newly-installed 5G satellite surveillance system, allowing centralised control of human thought, speech, writing and movement. Humans will be bar-coded to allow travel, work, and buying or selling. Immunisation is the preferred method of the Controllers to install the RFID chip, and 14 out of 17 goals of the *2030 UN Agenda for Sustainable Development* include immunisation. The immunisation (vaccination) record of a person is tracked via a micro-needle quantum dot tattoo on the person's skin. This highly specific medical record consists of copper-based quantum dots embedded in biocompatible micron-scale capsules. Their near-infrared dye is invisible, but the pattern they set can be read and interpreted by cell phone apps that shine near-infrared light onto the skin. After a period of about five years the tattoo would probably need to be renewed.

The mystic Rudolf Steiner foresaw this development relating to inoculation over a century ago. He wrote a series of essays at the end of 1917, published under the title *The Fall of the Spirits of Darkness,* in which he discussed the coming age of materialism and centralisation of power and control during which the influences of 'spirits of darkness' would inspire humans to devise new technologies and new means of oppression. With the arrival of the Covid-19 virus, 5G satellite surveillance technology and the RFID chip, humanity has reached that point. He said:

These innoculations will influence the human body in a way that will make it refuse to give a home to the spiritual inclinations of the soul. People will be inoculated against the inclination to entertain spiritual ideas....I have told you that the spirits of darkness are going to inspire their human hosts, in whom they will be dwelling, to find a vaccine that will drive all inclination towards spirituality out of people's souls when they are very young.

Incredibly, the Bible's *Book of Revelations* forewarns of this event relating to AI and RFID chips in humans. In fact, the *Book of Revelations* could be said to be a transhumanist document. At *Revelations* 3:2 and 3:3, it says to be watchful, and remember that we have been told what is happening. If you don't 'watch', in other words seek the knowledge and listen, the coming events will come "as a thief" and it will be sudden, with no ability to alter direction. We must listen and learn now before it is too late. At 13:16 and 13:17, it is stated that a mark will be placed on people's right hand (or forehead), and without the mark "no man will be able to buy or sell". At 16:2, it is stated that this mark will cause illness. At 20:4, it is stated that not receiving the mark may result in being killed for dissenting, but the souls of those who dissented will remain uncontaminated and linked to spirituality rather than materialism. *Revelations* say that these people will go to "the new earth". In taking the decision not to accept the mark, *Psalms* 9:10 specifically states that such a person will not be forsaken and abandoned.

The message in *Revelations* concerns the dangers of AI, and was a prophesy or warning relating to a time in the future when AI would be introduced on Earth. That time appears to be now. The warning from some unidentified already-knowledgeable high-tech source all those years ago when *Revelations* was written clearly indicates that transhumanism is not a good thing and will affect souls. *Revelations* states that it will take many centuries ("a thousand years") for those 'marked' souls to rectify the problems caused by AI (20:7).

The dangers of merging human consciousness with artificial intelligence are well portrayed in the films *Ex Machina* (2013) and *Ghost in the Shell* (2017). The future of humanity isn't human at all. The transhumanist agenda is the Controllers' 'end game', and it is here now.

It should always be remembered, however, that should dissention from this method of control by humanity's Controllers result in death, death is not

> the end, as this book shows. The soul is immortal, and should never be tampered with. In any event, the Controllers are in a race against time to control humanity, as a high-frequency event appears to be about to occur which is expected to resolve many people's dilemma about receiving the "mark of the beast". It is the event called Ascension (see Appendix 3).

In the end humans, however far they rise up the hierarchy of society, are still controlled by the "Controllers" in the current world structure. Life is always going to be precarious until we discover our true spiritual being and essence. What is clear is that the above principles for control over human beings have helped to keep people fighting, suffering, and dying for absolutely no good reason whatsoever.

ACKNOWLEDGEMENT

Thanks to Angel-Light Love, who is based in Dallas, Texas, a true healer and teacher, for her help in reviewing my many drafts of the book as it developed, and for her support over the years. She is someone who really understands the meaning of the words "service-to-others". Her Angel-Light Beamer blogs can be accessed at https://angel-light-love-healing.blogspot.com

BIBLIOGRAPHY

Alexander, Dr Eben – "Proof of Heaven"

Baldwin, William – "Healing Lost Souls"

Barham, Martha & Greene, James – "The Silver Cord: Lifeline to the Unobstructed"

Bauval, Robert & Gilbert, Adrian – "The Orion Mystery"

Bauval, Robert and Hancock, Graham – "The Master Game"

Begich, Nick and Manning, Jeane – "Angels Don't Play This HAARP"

Begich, Nick – "Controlling the Human Mind"

Black, Jonathan – "A Secret History of the World"

Bramley, William - "The Gods of Eden"

Brown, Dan – "The Lost Symbol"

Bruce, Robert – "The Practical Psychic Self-Defence Manual"

Calleman, Carl Johan – "The Mayan Calendar and the Transformation of Consciousness"

Cannon, Dolores – "The Convoluted Universe" (four volumes)

Cannon, Dolores – "The Custodians"

Cassidy, Kerry – "Rebel Gene"

Chatwin, Bruce – "The Songlines"

Cori, Patricia – "Cosmos of Soul"

Emoto, Dr Masaru – "The Hidden Messages in Water"

Gallup, George – "Adventures in Immortality"
Galouye, Daniel – "Simulacron-3"

Haich, Elizabeth – "Initiation"
Hancock, Graham – "Fingerprints of the Gods"
Hancock, Graham – "Supernatural"
Hartmann, Thom – "The Last Hours of Ancient Sunlight"
Hitchens, Christopher – "God is not Great"
Hodge, Stephen & Boord, Martin – "Tibetan Book of the Dead"
Howe, Linda Moulton – "Glimpses of Other Realities, Vol II: High Strangeness"

Icke, David – "Infinite Love is the Only Truth-Everything Else is Illusion"
Icke, David – "A Guide to the Global Conspiracy"
Icke, David – "Tales from the Time Loop"

Jacobs, David M. – "The Threat: Revealing the Secret Alien Agenda"
Joy, Karen – "Other Lives, Other Realms"

Kopel, Ari – "Getting Back to Source"
Kubler-Ross, Elizabeth – "On Life after Death"

Lachman, Gary – "Beyond the Robot" – The Life and Works of Colin Wilson
LaViolette, Paul – "Earth Under Fire"
Leininger, Bruce & Andrea, with Ken Gross – "Soul Survivor: The Reincarnation of a World War II Fighter Pilot"

Long, Jodie – "God's Fingerprints: Impressions of Near Death Experiences"

Martini, Richard – "Flipside: A Tourist's Guide on How To Navigate the Afterlife"
Matheson, Richard – "What Dreams May Come"
McTaggart, Lynne – "The Field"
McTaggart, Lynne – "The Intention Experiment"
Mirabello, Mark – "A Traveller's Guide to the Afterlife"
Monroe, Robert – "Far Journeys"
Monroe, Robert – "Life After Life"
Montaigne, David – "End Times and 2019"
Montaigne, David – "Pole Shift – Evidence will not be Silenced"
Moorjani, Anita – "Dying To Be Me"
Morris, Piers – "They Exist"
Morgan, Margo – "Mutant Message Down Under"
Myers, Frederick – "Human Personality and its Survival of Bodily Death"

Newton, Dr Michael – "Journey of Souls"
Newton, Dr Michael – "Destiny of Souls"
Newton, Dr Michael – "Life Between Lives"
Newton, Dr Michael – "Memories of the Afterlife"

Orwell, George – "1984"

Preston, Richard – "First Light"
Preston, Richard – "Hot Zone"
Pye, Lloyd – "Everything You Know is Wrong"

Rinpoche, Sogyal – "The Tibetan Book of Living and Dying"

Rodwell, Mary – "The New Human"

Sawyer, Karen – "A Dangerous Man"
Schuchard, Marsha Keith – "Why Mrs Blake Cried"
Shaw, George Bernard – "Back to Methuselah"
Shroder, Tom – "Old Souls"
Singer, Michael – "The Untethered Soul"
Snow, Dr Chet – "Mass Dreams of the Future"
Steiner, Rudolf – "Theosophy"

Talbot, Michael – "The Holographic Universe"
Tolle, Eckhart – "The Power of Now"
Tolle, Eckhart – "A New Earth"
Tucker, Jim – "Return to Life"
Turner, Dr Karla – "Taken – Inside the Alien-Human Abduction Agenda"

Walden, James – "The Ultimate Alien Agenda"
Walsch, Neale Donald – "Home With God"
Wambuch, Dr Helen – " Life Before Life"
Weiss, Dr Brian – "Many Lives, Many Masters"
Whitton, Joel L, MD and Fisher, Joe – "Life Between Life"
Wilcock, David – "The Source Field Investigations"
Wilcock, David – "The Synchronicity Key"
Wilcock, David – "The Ascension Mysteries"
Wilson, Colin – "Afterlife"
Wilson, Colin – "The Outsider"
Wilson, Colin – "Alien Dawn"
Wisehart, Susan – "Soul Visioning"

INDEX

Page

Lightning Source UK Ltd.
Milton Keynes UK
UKHW040730030921
389968UK00002B/334

9 781839 753060